To Ysha

For all the many years of debates

ACKNOWLEDGEMENTS

I would like to thank Michael York for not only introducing me to the thinking of chaos theory and complexity but for his enthusiasm in my pursuit of this subject. Similarly Patrick Curry added his challenging queries and philosophical insights which helped me forge the initial inspirations into a more meaningful argument. Additionally, my thanks also go to Nicolas Campion for the rolling debates on astrological history over pots of Earl Grey tea and to Irene Earis for her listening, insights and encouragement. Lastly I would like to acknowledge Darrelyn Gunzburg whose constant astute questions precipitated many new patterns in my mind.

CONTENTS

FOREWORD

Physics with Poetry, Science with Soul, Divination without the gods....

The discovery of Chaos theory and complexity have opened the mechanical eyes of science to a body of knowledge about which we have instinctively known since the dawn of time. By tripping over chaos, science fortuitously found some of the principles of the non-mechanical world: the world of the living and the world that supports the living. As a result, a new language has emerged which is being absorbed into the soft sciences such as psychology, sociology, and anthropology, a new language which is enabling these different bodies of knowledge to find a less ambiguous voice.

This new voice, I believe, can also provide fresh insights into the polarized debate on the role of astrology in Western culture. This debate on the very nature of astrology and its purpose has been oscillating between two fixed positions, one of which advocates that astrology belongs to the Newtonian paradigm and is a science which is still looking for its causal agent and the other, that astrology is a spiritual or divine subject. But this debate is effectively one about causal agents: the scientific position seeks a measurable cause while the spiritual position casts God or the gods in the role of the causal agent.

However, the findings of chaos theory and its cousin complexity science suggest a possible solution to this impasse, as they indicate a third orientation that does not require astrology to seek a causal agent, either physical or supernatural. Chaos thinking suggests that astrology may be able to take the best of both arguments, by providing it with a acceptable mainstream voice while at the same time allowing it to reserve its mystery and wonder through a form of divination, or pattern reading but *without* the causal gods.

In addition, separate to this debate, astrologers can use the new discoveries in chaos theory and complexity to revisit some of astrology's perennial questions such as, "What actually is astrology?", "Why is astrology so robust in our culture?", "Why is astrology so vilified?", as well as more philosophical questions such as, "What are the roles of fate, destiny and freewill that are implied by the horoscope?".

The act of visiting these questions is one of the themes of this work, yet in this journey we need to guard against over-enthusiasm. There is a saying that each generation gets the Stonehenge that it needs, a saying that recognises that the majestic megalithic site of stone and history on the Salisbury Plain in England is an enigma that reflects the current needs of the community. This metaphor also applies to astrology: each generation gains or creates the astrology that it needs or desires. So as Western culture moves away from seeing Newtonian science as the all powerful world view, the findings of chaos theory and complexity blended with astrology may seem, for some of us, a revelation. Yet this enthusiasm may wane when these insights are viewed from another time and in another place.

With this warning in mind, in the final chapter I have defined an astrological approach that I have labelled chaotic astrology. However, I am not seeking to turn astrology into an inferior or primitive sub-branch of chaos theory or complexity but simply adopting the practice of other subjects when they absorb chaos theory into their corpus, such as chaotic biology, chaotic economics, chaotic psychology, and the like. In defining and exploring the practice of chaotic astrology, it is my belief that many astrologers upon reading this work will find that their own philosophical approach to astrology is already chaotic[1]. In fact, to borrow from the French socialist Bruno Latour, I believe that astrology has never been modern, it has always been chaotic.

Finally this work is an introduction to the new ideas of chaos and complexity applied to the field of astrology. At the moment these ideas are largely theoretical and any empirical conclusions are drawn from my own practice as an astrologer. There is a great deal more research work required before we can, as a community, have real confidence in the weave astrology can make with chaos. Thus the aim of this little book is to simply present the idea of the potential for this weave so we can begin to explore divination without the gods.

Bernadette Brady
Bristol, UK
May, 2006

---

[1] see Phillipson, Gary.(2000). *Astrology in the Year Zero*. London: Flare Publications; Gunzburg, Darrelyn. (2004). *Life after Grief: An Astrological Guide to Dealing with Loss*. Bournemouth, UK: The Wessex Astrologer Ltd.

1

THE TWO WORLDS – COSMOS AND CHAOS

One of the first things I remember learning at school was that God made the world. This statement made up of four small words slid easily into my mind and became, unbeknown to me, the great foundation stone upon which I built all other things. At the time I did not understand the power of this statement for its awesomeness does not lie in majestic poetry or in the beauty of its language but rather in its implications. A clear logical Being decided to make the world. An artisan-God, a Being beyond being, designed, planned and engineered the world in which we live.

> In the beginning God created the heavens and the earth. The earth was without form and void and darkness was upon the face of the deep; and the Spirit of God was moving over the face of the waters.
>
> And God said, "Let there be light" and there was light, And God saw that the light was good; and God separated the light from the darkness. (*Genesis* 1:1-4) [1].

In this Biblical creation story one action logically follows another and each action provides the basis or cause for the next. In the beginning God creates light by separating it from

---

[1] *The Holy Bible*. (1972). Revised Standard Version. Nashville, USA: Nelson.

the darkness. This creates evening from which we have the first dawn. Having created the idea of day, God separates sky from earth and creates the heavens. On the second day He separates the waters of the earth to create land and creates the plant kingdom to grow upon the dry land. On the third day He creates the sun and the moon and the starry sky to act as signs for the seasons. On the fourth day God creates life in the seas and on the fifth day He creates life on dry land. On the sixth day God creates man in His image and gives him rulership over all of his creations. On the seventh day He rests, giving to His new found order the concept of a holy day.

This story tells us that creation is driven by a single mind with a clear plan. The plan is implemented methodically step by step, and as each step is put into place, this mind places a value judgment on His work. Right from the beginning of this creation myth, the creative force of Order announces that the light is good and, by inference, that the dark is bad and to be avoided. It is a powerful story because it tells us the way in which things happen in our world, the world made by an artisan-God. It tells us that the world was created in a logical causal manner and all new order which is created in this world will therefore also be produced in a logical linear causal manner. So in this world in which I thought I lived, all things could only be logical, all things had to have a cause which could be discovered and if some order did not have a causal agent, then it was not actually order but simply an illusion.

The fact that my grandmother would always seem to know when something was going to happen had no rational or logical explanation and no causal agent, thus it was my family's delusional misunderstanding of a series of flukes.

The fact that my uncle won the State lotto on three separate occasions was just an amazing coincidence, as there was no such thing as a "lucky" person.

The fact that the eldest son of most branches of my family, had over many generations, fallen mortally ill in their youth and had only been saved at death's door by desperate prayer and a last attempt "my God nothing else is working" holy relic was simply one of life's little funny things which had no meaning, an odd coincidence for my family, without pattern.

The world was a logical, orderly place. It was created by an expression of Order (God) and would continue to function in this manner for all time.

As I grew older, ignoring the evidence of the layers of Celtic mysticism that ran through my family, I learnt that life on earth was started by a chemical accident and from that first "accident", by trial and error and through the mechanism of survival of the fittest, all the diversity of life on this planet slowly evolved. At the same time as I was eating Charles Darwin's theory of evolution for breakfast, I learnt that the world was created by the big bang, a blinding flash of creation that has been fuelling the whole universe from that moment forward.

I do remember having one bad day at school somewhere between a science lesson and walking to a religious doctrine class where the big bang and Darwin seemed to clash with the great foundation stone statement of "God made the world". However, although it caused a ruffle to my thinking around the question of who actually was responsible for making the world, in the end, accepting the big bang merely needed me to rearrange some of the chess pieces of my mind. Both stories had the same meaning – someone or something made the world. Once the world or the universe was made on that first day of creation, whether it was through the big bang between 13 billion and 20 billon years ago or whether it was the *Genesis* version of

Sunday, 23 October, 4004 B.C.E.[2], then everything that I could see, everything that made up the earth and the stars and the heavens was the logical result of an earlier action. The world was still like a machine still bolted together but now not only by God but by God through Newton's gravity and Darwin's theory of evolution.

My creation myth was left intact and still located me in a causal linear world. We all need a creation myth and we all have one, the great foundation stone on which we consciously or unconsciously build our expectations of our world – its limits and what can and cannot happen. It did not worry me too much that both *Genesis* and the big bang left a lot of things unexplained. Such as the odd repeating events in my family history that did seem to have meaning even if my world view said they did not. There was also the evidence of my grandmother's "sight" and the power of dreams, the feeling of a house – good or bad – not to mention the way the family dogs howled before someone died. However, all of that had to be put to one side, labelled as irrelevant silliness, for in the eyes of a world made by Order, my irrational, illogical family stories were simply a delusion. Whether you are aware of it or not, your creation myth is the companion that walks with you all the days of your life, a companion who labels all things in your world as either rational and correct or irrational and therefore illusional.

For example, if one's creation myth is biblical and reflects *Genesis*, then all things are measured according to this story. If you believe, for example, that God made the world in seven days and then made man in his image[3], then you will assume

---

[2] Andrew D. White. (1897). *A History of the Warfare of Science with Theology in Christendom*. London, UK:D. Appleton and Co:9.
[3] God made man not woman in his image, so the use of the masculine pronoun is appropriate.

that man has a special relationship to God and man is therefore at the top of a hierarchically constructed nature. God and man look the same. However, the reality of this myth is that God is made in man's image and this means that man assumes himself to be the superior life force on the planet. With this creation myth mankind, by divine right, can treat all other expressions of creation as objects that exist purely to serve his or we could say His desire, for in this creation myth Man is god. If you believe in the more modern version of this myth, that the universe began at the moment of a big bang and from that time forward the force of this great creative explosion has been the ultimate force behind all other events, then, interestingly the same world view can be generated.

Both these models of creation are linear, with timelines moving forward in one single direction, relentlessly pushed along by an initial starting force. In *Genesis* God creates the world after which He appears to leave it to run its course, the slow disintegration from an originally pure form. The big bang suggests a universe progressively winding down to a cold soup of total uniformity. Both these creation myths have an external force "pushing" the world into being. In *Genesis* this force is the hand of an artisan God; in the big bang the engine room of creation is the force of the explosion. Both these ideas about creation are causal and linear and shape our minds to only see a causal and linear world.

Like most people, I grew up in this causal linear world view, but my family's daily life with its repetitive generational stories and the constant menu of superstitious beliefs – don't let any knives cross each other at the dinner table, always buy parsley, never accept it as a gift, never bury the dead without a coin for the ferryman – along with the personal ritual practices of carrying a token for luck or protection, wishing on the new moon, and seeing a small event as an omen of a larger one, all acted like quicksand to the granite foundations of my causal creation myth. Eventually, and quite by chance, I found myself thinking beyond the walled garden of my ordered world. I dared to think that maybe the way my family lived was not mad, silly and "just" a delusion. I started to study astrology and walked through a gate which had a large sign hanging over it which read: "Danger! Primitive ignorant beliefs lie beyond this point". I moved beyond the walls of the causal garden and into an un-named place that was not defined by any creation myth I understood; for my new interest, astrology, unbeknown to me at that time had emerged in the human mind well before the biblical creation myth of *Genesis* was written down, and before the theory of the big bang. It emerged, in fact, before our creation myths were linear and causal.

It may come as a surprise to some but the world has not always been as it is. There have been other ways of knowing and other ways of thinking, other ways of living in the world and indeed even other worlds in which to live. Four thousand years ago, at the time of the emergence of astrology in the human mind, a very different world was in force and this ancient world can be glimpsed in its creation myths. These early creation myths, just like our modern version, are like blueprints of an earlier time. Traditionally modern Western culture has viewed these earlier creation myths as dusty artefacts in the museum of our thinking, worthy only of being exhibited as curiosities and dismissed as the products of primitive or ignorant minds. But they are not; they are windows into a lost world.

We group creation myths under such labels as primordial, religious, or modern and scientific, and we assume that the most recent, our own, is the correct myth, the truth of how our world came into being and how it works. We also tend to think of creation myths as exclusive, as if there is only ever one *real* way our world came into existence. Stray artefacts from other older creation myths or simply things which are not explained by the current myth are viewed as ignorance, superstition or delusional ideas by the modern world. Yet despite such labels, such myth-fragments or unexplained debris do tend to drift into our lives and it seemed to me to be not just within my own family's story but almost everywhere I looked. People from all walks of life talked of their superstitions, serendipities of life and "strange" events but only labelled as "strange" as they had no place in the modern ordered logical creation myth.

The Australian cricket captain, Steve Waugh (Captain 1999-2005), who set new world records in batting, never went out to the wicket without his old red handkerchief showing against his cricket whites. This was his superstition, his personal ritual, for the story goes that he had initially carried that red handkerchief on a day when he had scored well. Cricket commentators would watch for it as he came out to bat to ensure that all was well and eventually its growing ragged and faded appearance became a measure of the length of his successful career. We could dismiss Steve Waugh's superstition around his red handkerchief by suggesting that its presence simply put him in a better mental space for achieving a high score, but it was Steve Waugh's belief in the power of his old red handkerchief which showed his belief in another world. This belief was not, however, just peculiar to him as it was also shared with thousands of Australian cricket fans, all of them wanting to know if his red handkerchief was in his pocket and thus also showing their belief in a world beyond the walled garden of order and logic.

Placed in the context of our modern scientific understanding of the creation of order, these beliefs - my family's ideas on the meaning of coincidences and Steve Waugh's (and the cricket fans') belief in that old red handkerchief - actually contradicts the accepted ideas of the origin of order (how things happen) and therefore these beliefs are judged as delusional or foolish. Yet if we put these beliefs into the framework of older creation myths (other ideas on how things happen), then my family's recognition of superstitions and patterns and the actions of the superstitious cricketer seem logical. So what is this world that we have been taught not to see?

Stories from beyond the Walled Garden

These earlier creation myths talk of the need to return to a creative void. They are cyclic and repetitive and it is reasonable to assume that creation myths of this kind were built neither on religious doctrine nor on technological theory but rather appear to have emerged from the observation of the workings of life itself, the way we experience the day to day living of our lives: day and night, seasons following seasons, routines, rituals and patterns, and life and death.

In one of the creation myths from the Australian aborigines there is the theme of a void, an intention-filled nothingness from which patterns of life emerge and return and emerge again, half-formed, half-shaped until finally their form is found. The Australian aborigines call this the Time of the Dreaming.

> In the beginning the earth was a bare plain. All was dark. There was no life, no death. The sun, the moon, and the stars slept beneath the earth. All the eternal ancestors slept there, too, until at last they woke themselves out of their own eternity and broke through to the surface. When the eternal ancestors arose, in the Dreamtime, they wandered the earth, sometimes in animal form - as kangaroos, or emus, or lizards - sometimes in human shape, sometimes part animal and human, sometimes as part human and plant.

Two such beings, self-created out of nothing, were the Ungambikula. Wandering the world, they found half-made human beings. They were made of animals and plants, but were shapeless bundles, lying higgledy-piggledy, near where water holes and salt lakes could be created. The people were all doubled over into balls, vague and unfinished, without limbs or features. With their great stone knives, the Ungambikula carved heads, bodies, legs, and arms out of the bundles. They made the faces, and the hands and feet. At last the human beings were finished[4].

Another example of a cyclic creation myth comes from China:

In the beginning there was darkness everywhere, and Chaos ruled. Within the darkness there formed an egg, and inside the egg the giant Pangu came into being. For aeons, safely inside the egg, Pangu slept and grew. When he had grown to gigantic size he stretched his huge limbs and in so doing broke the egg. The lighter parts of the egg floated upwards to form the heavens and the denser parts sank downwards, to become the earth. And so was formed earth and sky, Yin and Yang.

Pangu saw what had happened and he was pleased. But he feared that heaven and earth might meld together again, so he placed himself between them, his head holding up the sky and his feet firmly upon the earth. Pangu continued to grow at a rate of ten feet a day for 18,000 years, so increasing the distance between heaven and earth, until they seemed fixed and secure, 30,000 miles apart. Now exhausted, Pangu went back to sleep and never woke up.

---

[4] Australian Aborigine myths - http://www.dreamscape.com/morgana/ miranda.htm#AUS   Accessed 30 September, 2004.

Pangu died, and his body went to make the world and all its elements. The wind and clouds were formed from his breath, his voice was thunder and lightning, his eyes became the sun and moon, his arms and his legs became the four directions of the compass and his trunk became the mountains. His flesh turned into the soil and the trees that grow on it, his blood into the rivers that flow and his veins into paths men travel. His body hair became the grass and herbs, and his skin the same, while precious stones and minerals were formed from his bones and teeth. His sweat became the dew and the hair of his head became the stars that trail throughout heaven. As for the parasites on his body, these became the different races of humankind.[5]

From the gentle Pangu, we can turn to the Egyptians. The pyramid texts from around the middle of the 3rd millennium B.C.E. talk of a watery expanse with no beginning and no end, a primordial entity, an inert principle which contained within itself all possibilities[6].

Before sky existed, before earth existed, before men existed, before death existed.[7]

The Egyptians knew this place as Nun and from its swirling waters which stirred the river silt, the ram-headed Khnum emerged, like the Ungambikula of the dreamtime. His emergence was known as the First Occasion and once emerged Khnum, in the form of a potter, began to create the rest of life, dipping his hand or his pot, into the silt of the Nile and shaping all life on his wheel. He is a polymorphic water deity who is

---

[5]   Chinese myths - http://www.dreamscape.com/morgana/ariel.htm#HAW Accessed 30 September, 2004.

[6]   Francoise Dunand and Christiane Zivie-Coche. (2004). *Gods and Men in Egypt, 3000 BCE to 395 CE*. London, UK: Connell University Press:46.

[7]   Pyramid Texts spell 571, 1466.

called Father of Fathers and Mother of Mothers and is depicted both with a potter's wheel and also with a large water jug, an image which indicates that he is probably the source of the imagery of the constellation of Aquarius[8].

Figure 1 – The ram-headed Khnum, the potter. He is a polymorphic deity known as Father of Fathers and Mother of Mothers and is considered to be one of the earliest Egyptian deities established in the Predynastic Period (5464 – 3414 B.C.E.). He emerged from the void (Nun) and then proceeded to create the rest of life on his potter's wheel.

For the Egyptians, Order or the known world emerged from the void of Nun, not once, not twice but many times. The first time was called the First Occasion but from that point forward the First Occasion was revisited and repeated. The First Occasion occurred with every dawn, with every Nile flood, and with every new pharaoh. History for the Egyptians was

[8] For more information see Bernadette Brady. (1998) *Brady's Book of Fixed Stars*. Maine, USA: Samuel Weiser:305.

not a timeline stretching back to some agreed single starting point and marching steadily forward, containing within its dates the history, weight and guilt of a never-ending linear journey. The Egyptians measured their years from the time of the current pharaoh, the time of that *particular* First Occasion, and temples were torn down with no thought to their history, for history was temporal and cyclic and it was only correct to once again re-engage with the First Occasion[9].

The Greeks also acknowledge the void in their creation myth but revealingly they are less concerned with cycles. Their oldest known version was written down by Hesiod in the *Theogony* around 700 B.C.E.

> Verily at the first Chaos came to be, but next wide-bosomed Earth [Gaia], the ever-sure foundations of all the deathless ones who hold the peaks of snowy Olympus, and dim Tartarus in the depth of the wide-pathed Gaea, and Eros (Love), fairest among the deathless gods, who unnerves the limbs and overcomes the mind and wise counsels of all gods and all men within them.

> From Chaos came forth Erebus and black Night; but of Night were born Aether and Day, whom she conceived and bare from union in love with Erebus. And Earth first bare starry Heaven, equal to herself, to cover her on every side, and to be an ever-sure abiding-place for the blessed gods. And she brought forth long Hills, graceful haunts of the goddess-Nymphs who dwell amongst the glens of the hills. She bare also the fruitless deep with his raging swell, Pontus, without sweet union of love[10].

---

[9] F. Dunand and C. Zivie-Coche. *Gods and Men in Egypt, 3000 BCE to 395 CE*: 66.

[10] Hesiod, *The Theogony* - http://omacl.org/Hesiod/theogony.html. Accessed 30 March 2006.

The myth continues with Gaia lying with the starry sky and giving birth to the Titans and, "After them [the Titans] was born Cronos the wily, youngest and most terrible of her children, and he hated his lusty sire".

In these creation myths chaos or the void is an essential state for the creation of new forms. The Ungambikula emerge and help shape the other humans. Pangu emerges and separates the earth from the sky. Eventually he returns to the chaotic void by dying and his decomposing body becomes the *prima materia* of creation. In the Egyptian myth a potter emerges from Nun and dips his hand into the silt of Nile and begins to shape life on his wheel and in the Greek myth which has many generations but still begins with Chaos, Gaia emerges and gives birth to Night and Erebus. The chaos in these myths is not a place of emptiness, it is not a place of "nothing" but a place containing an unconscious, unseen, underlying order, the potential to spontaneously produce a pattern, a place or a state that produces life[11].

The world defined by chaotic creation myths

If the causal linear myths of *Genesis* and the big bang impose the rigours of logic, cause and effect, and machine-like order on the world, then what are the "rules" of a world defined by chaotic creation myths? What does the Egyptian idea of the return to the First Occasion tell us about their world, their expectations, their ideas about what can happen and what cannot happen? What does the death of Pangu tell us about the Chinese world view?

---

[11] see: J.Briggs and F.D. Peat. (1989). *The turbulent mirror: An illustrated guide to chaos theory and the science of wholeness*. New York: Harper & Row; James Gleick. (1987). *Chaos: making a new science*. New York: Viking-Penguin; Michael Butz. (1997). *Chaos and Complexity – Implications for Psychological Theory and Practice*. Washington, DC, USA: Taylor and Francis. 207,209.

Canadian anthropologist Sean Kane talks of the myths from many pre-history cultures as being stories of patterns, stories which talk of the relationships between plants, animals and earth where humanity is not central but one of many players in the unfolding patterns of life[12]. Indeed one of the most notable features of chaotic creation myths is that they emerge without an anthropological agenda and do not favour humanity over other forms of life. The divine is represented in many different guises, with gods and goddesses being part of the landscape as mountains or rivers, plants or animals or polymorphic mixtures of plant, animal and human. Creation in these myths is order-centred not human-centred, focused on creating the *whole* ordered world, an interlinked web of relationships and patterns, signs and events, symbols and corresponding implications. Into this rich web of relationships and interconnectedness every shape of nature holds divinity, residing in an eagle, a mountain, a human being, or a sky, for the chaotic world was and still is full of many voices.

We can see this diversity in artefacts from these worlds. *The Goddess of Lespugue (see figure 2)* is a statue made some 23,000 years ago where the "goddess" has a bird-like head with an egg shaped body. She is neither human nor bird, nor is she egg; rather she is a blended mixture of all three.

In Mesopotamia around 1800 B.C.E. such polymorphic blends of human, plant and animal or half formed or shape-changed humans can also be seen in *The Queen of the Night (see figure 3)* where the goddess has human form but is winged and has the feet of a bird. From such images, and the iconography of Egypt is full of them, we can see a chaotic and pluralist world that has humans as one of the characters in the unfolding narratives but not as the central dominating supreme entity.

---

[12] Sean A.Kane.(1998). *Wisdom of the Mythtellers*. Ontario, Canada: Broadview:36.

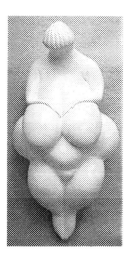

Figure 2 - 23,000 B.C. E. –
The Goddess of Lespugue.
Found standing on a
hearthstone in a shallow
cave in the Pyrenees of
southern France. The
mammoth ivory original is 5
3/4 inches tall, and is now in
the Musee L'Homme, France.
It is from the Gravettian-
Upper Perigordian of about
23,000 B.C.E.

Figure 3 - 1800-1750 B.C.E. -
The Queen of the Night - Old
Babylonian, from southern
Iraq. The figure of the
curvaceous naked woman
wears the horned headdress
characteristic of a
Mesopotamian deity and holds
a rod and ring of justice,
symbols of her divinity. Her
long multi-coloured wings
hang downwards, indicating
that she is a goddess of the
Underworld. Her legs end in
the talons of a bird of prey,
similar to those of the two owls
that flank her. She stands on
the backs of two lions and a
scale pattern indicates
mountains.

Another feature of these myths is that the polymorphic divine beings emerge half formed from the void and then help other life forms to be created. They pull them from the mud, shape them with their hands or, as in the Chinese example, produce them from their decaying body. These divine forms are themselves children of the void and the whole process is of emergences and return, emergences and return, over and over. It is a ballet of co-creation between the divine and the rest of life with the divine creating life and life creating the divine in a cyclic never ending rhythm, for chaotic creation myths are cyclic rather than linear.

But even if we can, from our modern perspective, accept the idea of the first divine entity being just one of the forms created from the void, the other major principle of these myths is so alien to our causal linear world view that we can almost miss it. It is that the source of new order is not causal and logical but rather it spontaneously emerges from the void. Order is not created by an artisan entity thinking about what to design today but rather is a natural expression of a relationship-rich, womb-like void. Once the new order has emerged an artisan can work with it to pull it from the void, but its first shape is a spontaneous event, like an idea emerging in your mind – it cannot be forced but once present can be developed into a clearer form.

So let us explore this notion and look at the world beyond the walled garden.

Whether we can accept this idea of creation or not, we can see from these early creation myths that it was the world view of our ancestors. Order was seen to emerge from a relationship-rich and unpredictable intention-filled void. This order was not only the order of the stability of the kingdom, such as the times of plenty, the life giving rains or the healthy birth of a child; it was also the emerging order that could destabilise the kingdom, a storm, a possible attack from one's enemies, a time of famine or flood. All of these events were considered a form of order which emerged spontaneously from the void. The potential impact of these events on every day life motivated our ancestors to search for ways of understanding, controlling or even influencing the new emerging order.

With all of life and the entire known world thought to be interlinked, this ambition took the form of looking for any early indications of new emergent order. The first glimmers of such a pattern could therefore show itself in the changing patterns of clouds or the swirling flight of a flock of birds or dreams or the behaviour of the wandering planets through the starry sky. Once such a pattern-sensitive palette was found it could then be studied, recorded, compared, and most importantly watched to seek "news" from the void, information regarding the forthcoming new order.

When an event was observed on the chosen palette and a connection to a second event made, one could use this knowledge to watch for, or even intentionally recreate via ritual, the first event in order to predict or stimulate the second event. The simplest expression of this pattern watching venture was omens - two events which were linked in some way so that one event reflected information concerning the other. The pair of events which make up an omen consists of the protasis (if-cause) and the apodosis (the forecast) [13]. For example, in a translation of a Babylonian Venus omen from the 7th century B.C.E. we have:

> "If Venus's position is green: pregnant women will die with their foetuses – Saturn stands with her."[14]

---

[13] Erica Reiner. (1999). "Babylonian Celestial Divination", in *Ancient Astronomy and Celestial Divination* (ed) Swerdlow, N.M. London: MIT Press. 21– 37: 23.

[14] ibid p.33.

This is a celestial omen linking a visual event in the sky – the protasis - with predicting a human event on earth – the apodosis. Furthermore, within the nature of omens and superstition, if the protasis was repeated or, in the case of different protasis, could be repeated in the form of personal or public ritual, then one could expect the apodosis to be repeated in a similar manner.

This is the philosophy underpinning Steve Waugh's red handkerchief, indeed this is the "logic" behind all superstitions. One event occurs marking the potential of another event or we can consciously create one event (carry the lucky handkerchief) in the hope of stimulating from the void the emergence of another event (a high cricket score).

Ritual and repetition in the chaotic paradigm

These earlier creation myths imply that we actually live inside creation and that we are a part of a relationship-rich pattern which is co-creating the web of life. Thus all of life, including humankind, has an important role to play in the co-creation of order and the health of one's environment. In these myths humans are not outside the system using the world like a construction site but rather we are inside the "fish bowl" with the rest of life. And when you are simply one of the "fishes" co-creating with an emergent potential (the void), then apart from watching for the first early signs of new emergent patterns, a practical approach was to also find some way to either maintain the order that has emerged, discourage any unwanted order from emerging, or seek to encourage the emergence of new desired order.

The principle tool the Egyptians used to maintain this all-important order was, as with other cultures, the act of ritual. Ritual was a tool, a practical instrument used to work with the emergent order and coax it from the void. Ritual was thought to be the way to stir the "silt of the Nile" and encourage the emergence of new patterns which Khnum, having already emerged, could then mould on his potter's wheel.

This vital relationship of ritual to order is seen in the role of the Egyptian temple. These were not houses of worship for the common masses with an Egyptian priest responsible for a "parish" which he tended with loving compassion for the humble lives of his people. In fact, the general population was unwelcome there for the temples were the houses or private residences of the gods, not the "house of God" of the modern day church. The temple's relationship to its "flock" was simply to collect worldly goods so it could maintain itself and the role of the priest was to perform the services which would maintain the well-being of the gods, much like a servant in a noble household. The physical images of the gods were a symbol of the order and patterns that had emerged from the void and maintaining the gods perpetuated this order. The daily and annual rituals performed by the priest were considered vital for ensuring the order of the kingdom in the same way as today's daily stock market trading rituals are considered vital for the stability and order of our modern world.

As ritual was required to ensure the perpetuation of order, it was necessary at both the public as well as personal levels of life. The noblest aspiration of an Egyptian was to live the life of the "silent man", in harmony with the seasons, maintaining regular patterns of behaviour, keeping the way of Maat and thereby actively contributing to the annual flooding of the Nile and the success and fruitfulness of the kingdom[15]. The relationship that life had to the emerging order was to reproduce repeating cycles to encourage the order to be maintained. Nature did this, the seasons did this and human life was expected to do this, also. Chaotic creation myths

---

[15] Henri Frankfort. (1956). *The Birth of Civilization in the Near East.* New York:Double Day:104.

indicated that ritual applied as an active principle to the void of chaos helped shape the emerging order. Ritual then applied to a established order ensured that the emergent order did not return to chaos.

We see further examples of how ritual maintained the order and stability of the kingdom in Babylonian beliefs. In a letter written by Akkaullanu, an Assyrian priest, to his king Esarhaddon (681 – 669 B.C.E.), Akkaullanu shows his frustration and fear, as the king has not performed the correct rituals for maintaining order in the face of a forthcoming eclipse.

> … As regards the substitute statue about which the king my lord, wrote to his servant: "It was sitting in the city of Akkad from the 14th of Duuzu till the 5th of Abu", And why did they enthrone it in A k k a d[16] [sic]? Should they have done it in the city of your father where you yourself are living, it would have removed your evil! Why y o u [sic] ? And why an evil of A k k a d [sic] ? Have they perhaps said to you on this matter: "Your father enthroned his substitutes there". These talks are rubbish! Why did the king not say to them like this: "The evil of my father was in one region, mine is in another one; the evil of Assyria and Akkad are not identical?: when a sign pertaining to Assyria appears, the ritual should be performed here, and when a sign pertaining to Akkad appears, it should be done there." Now the king of Akkad is well![17]

The priest continues his lament against the king, providing some hope for the situation by saying: "If the planet Jupiter is present in the eclipse, all is well with the king, a noble dignity will die in his stead." But order had surely been threatened by

---

[16] The priest's manner of writing the name of the city "Akkad" and the word "you" may be a form of stressing the word.
[17] Simo Parpola. (1970). *Letters from Assyrian Scholars to the Kings Esarhaddon and Assurbanipal Part 1*. Germany: Butzon and Kevelaer : 255.

incorrect ritual and the incompetent staff in charge of the substitute statue.

Ritual, here can be seen as any conscious act of repetition for the purpose to either maintaining a smooth continuum or to help create a better situation and as such was central to the chaotic world. Humans, like other parts of nature, had rituals to perform. Each ritual was just as important as the next and each perpetual return lead to maintaining the sacred order of life on earth[18].

Indeed omens, superstitions and the need for ritual, judged by our modern world to be primitive and the result of ignorance, are in fact valid and "logical" tools which belong to this other view of creation. This is the world that links events and/or objects and patterns: a red handkerchief and high batting scores, a green Venus and the death of pregnant women, or a broken mirror and bad luck; and each time the believer expects the recurrence of a type of order based on the repeating themes of another type of order or emerging pattern.

In this world, the one outside the walled garden of causal linear logic, I could dare to ask the question as to why the eldest sons in the different branches of my family needed to face death in their youth. I might not find an easy answer but I could at least ask the question.

Astrology and the world beyond the Walled Garden

The fact which seems to have been forgotten by both astrologers as well as their critics is that astrology, broadly defined as the practice of reading celestial omens, had its origin at the time when creation was linked to the void. It is commonly accepted that astrology developed in a visual format in Mesopotamia in the third millennium B.C.E. The visual world was read as a flowing, interchanging relationship

---

[18] S.A.Kane. *Wisdom of the Mythtellers*:14.

between the earth and the sky and astrology was the practice of interpreting that blended mixture[19]. James Tester refers to the Babylonians of the second millennium B.C.E. in the following way:

> They clearly presupposed that there is some relationship between what happens in the sky and what happens on earth, though they do not suggest that the relationship is one of cause and effect[20].

Here Tester implies, although not necessarily intentionally, that the Babylonian world view was based on what we now define as the chaotic paradigm where creation comes from the void, and order emerges *without* a linear causal agent. The Babylonians sought to understand the unfolding emerging patterns of events of life on earth through the mixture of celestial phenomena, weather patterns and omens[21]. It is logical that a culture who watched the sky and recorded events in an effort to understand their turbulent world would develop an early form of astrology. Indeed it is only within the environment of such a chaotic philosophy that astrology could have emerged, for it assumes that one can read order and understand patterns of events on earth by observing the complex and numerous variables within the heavens[22].

---

[19] Nicholas Campion. (1982). *An introduction to the history of astrology*. London: ISCWA: 7; Erica Reiner. "Babylonian Celestial Divination": 22.

[20] Jim Tester. (1987). *A History of Western Astrology*. Woodbridge, UK:The Boydell Press:13.

[21] C.B.F Walker.(1989). "A sketch of the development of Mesopotamian astrology and horoscopes." in *History and Astrology*. (ed) Kitson, Annabella. London: Uwin Paperbacks: 7-14.

[22] Claudius Ptolemy. (1969). *The Tetrabiblos*. (Trans) Ashmand. J. M. Mokelumne Hill, USA: Health Research:2; Jean-Baptiste Morin. (1994). *Astrologia Gallica Book Twenty-Two Directions*. (Trans) Holden, James. Tempe, USA: AFA :7.

So the world defined by chaotic creation myths is vastly different from the one in which we think we live. Not only does the chaotic world function differently, create order differently in a way that does not require logical causality, it also holds vastly different beliefs, vastly different expectations and vastly different definitions of the divine. In short the chaotic world functions as if all things were inter-related and dictates that it is better to live in harmony with the world in order to maintain the precious order which has emerged. Part of this harmony was the need to respect the daily or public rituals which help to maintain society, while at the same time one should be vigilant to watch for the first signs of the beginnings of new events, new ideas or new threats. These new incoming events could be first noticed in dreams or the shape of clouds, or the flight of birds or the movement of the planets amongst the stars.

The Walled Garden – a desire to be separate

This void, this intention-filled nothingness, which was honoured in myths from Egypt, China, Greece and the Australian aboriginal dreamtime, received a manifestly different treatment in the Babylonian creation myth. The Fertile Crescent was a land of war and battle and from this insecure place we gained a different version of creation from the void. First recorded in the 12th century B.C.E, the *Enuma Elish* is thought to be an older Sumerian story and, like the Egyptian myth, it begins with the mixing of waters – sweet water and bitter water. Like other creation myths from this period, the stirring of the water creates life – Apsu and Tiamat, husband and wife:

> When there was no heaven,
> no earth, no height, no depth, no name,
> when Apsu was alone,
> the sweet water, the first begetter; and Tiamat

the bitter water, and that
return to the womb, her Mummu,
when there were no gods-

When sweet and bitter
mingled together, no reed was plaited, no rushes
muddied the water,
the gods were nameless, natureless, futureless, then
from Apsu and Tiamat
in the waters gods were created, in the waters
silt precipitated.[23]

It is a great epic and further god-children are created by these mingling of waters. But in this myth when the natural cyclic pull to return to the chaotic state begins, as personified by Apsu's desire to remake his children, they resist and fight their "terrible" father. Finding no other solution to the irresistible pull back into the void, the children who represent new-formed order use spells to kill their father. Much later this same tension is represented in the story of the Greek god Cronos who returns his children to the void by eating them but when he is fed a magic potion, he simply vomits them back into life. Cronos then becomes the central figure in a battle against the newly emergent children. However, in the earlier Babylonian myth it is Tiamat, the wife of the murdered Apsu and the bitter water of the void, who becomes the great enemy. She, Tiamat, fights her children.

This war is at the heart of the *Enuma Elish*. It is a conflict between the self-awareness of Order fighting any inclination to return to Chaos. In this Babylonian myth, believed to be one of the major sources for the Christian *Genesis*, order (children) fight with chaos (Tiamat) to resist re-absorption. This is an important myth as it captures the early signs of the

[23] L.W. King.(1902) 2004. *The Seven Tablets of Creation: The Babylonian and Assyrian Legends Concerning the Creation of the World and of Mankind.* Montana, USA: Kessinger Publishing.

shift of thinking from the chaotic ideas of creation to the causal view. In this myth we see humans wishing to be separate to the rest of creation, as they seek to resist absorption, they seek to resist death. Yet even though this creation myth is full of conflict, it still contains the two vital components of creation: the creative void and the consciousness of order; sleep and wakefulness, dreams and corporeal, virtual and real, life and death.

The Removal of the eighth day – an end to cycles

The *Enuma Elish* went through a major rewrite in the 6th or 5th century B.C.E.[24] The desire of Order to permanently separate itself from the creative void resulted in a redefinition of the void. In the new, rewritten myth, the void changed from an intent-rich place, pregnant with the *prima materia* of all life to a place of neutral nothingness, a void with no material substance. No longer was it the silt of the Nile, or clay on a potter's wheel. In this rewritten myth the void was an empty place, and a single conscious mind (Order) delved into the nothingness and created the world in its own vision. No longer did the mingling waters swirl the silt to form the first patterns of life.

Removing the creative void and replacing it with a conscious designer was a major paradigm shift. Now the causal linear world was the sole source of creation. God never needed to remake this new world for in this evolutional, methodical, linear approach to creation there is *no* cyclic return because there is *no* void and so no threat of disorder. There are in fact no cycles in this new myth for cycles are the way in which one is returned to the void. The artisan God (Order), having created more Order (the world), considers that Order is a

---

[24] R.E. Friedman.(1997). *Who Wrote the Bible?* San Francisco: HarperCollins: 246-247.

permanent state. In this myth which we know as *Genesis*, God stops work on the seventh day, there is no eighth day of creation for Order is forever. Death or the void is removed and replaced by an immortal life in *paradise* (the Greek word for a walled garden).

The Greeks named this order which was created by Order as *ko'smos* and their view of "cosmos" was the glorification of this self-creating Order. *Ex nihilo nihil fit* – nothing comes from nothing – was the insult that the Greeks threw at the old idea of creation coming from the void. They loathed the older idea of *creatio ex nihilo* – creation out of nothing – which was at the heart of the Egyptian and earlier ideas of creation as it inhibited them from building causal linear knowledge. The chaotician Ralph Abraham defines these *ex nihilo nihil fit* creation myths as the theory of origin from order and labels them cosmic creation myths or the cosmic paradigm[25].

So the chaotic view of a world made of cycles in a flowing balance between order and the creative void was cast aside. These creation myths, and thus the world view and philosophical environment which gave rise to the emergence of astrology, omens, divination and the like, were all disregarded. The knowledge-hungry Greeks adopted and supported the themes of a cosmic creation myth because it gave them an intellectual position from which they could analyse the world - linear causality. Their resulting philosophies cemented linear causality into the Western mind and from this new position humanity could strive to imitate the artisan God and use nature like a construction site.

---

[25]   R. Abraham (1994). *Chaos, Gaia, Eros*. New York: HarperSanFrancisco :125.

With this construction site attitude we have been able to achieve many things for it has allowed us to discover the mechanical properties of physical matter and to produce technological miracles. Additionally, by embracing this myth of linear creation, we adopted the world view that all events were *only* the logical extensions of another earlier event and thus could be totally understood as a series of separate incidents. This breathtakingly simplistic view enabled us to ignore the importance of the multiplicity of relationships in our environment and thus blinded us to its delicate balance. In this causal creation myth we are separate entities moving forward on an evolutional path of constant improvement towards a new and glorious age which some believe to be the promised second coming of Christ, the Kingdom of God, seen as the ultimate expression of Order.

Now if you are lucky enough to be born as a member of this God-race, the cosmic paradigm is most seductive. We are allowed to live outside of and separate to the web of life, in control of the entire world with the rest of nature being our playground. We do not need to be concerned with consequences because there are none – no void, no disorder. Additionally we and we alone are promised the ultimate prize of paradise or heaven. Life is indeed good inside the walled garden even if you have to ignore all the pattern rich, interrelated serendipities of life, even if you have to live in a world where your dreams have no meaning and you have to accept that your beloved dog or cat will not meet you in paradise because they are not lucky enough to be a member of the God-race.

The cosmic creation myth is perfect for the world of unique objects but is the cosmic creation myth appropriate for living systems? Is it possible to live in both worlds, that of cosmic – the world of objects – as well as the chaotic, the world of the living, the world of coincidences and meaningful family patterns?

If it is possible to live in both worlds then why does the cosmic world demand that no other world exist? Why are we not meant to leave the walled garden?

The world of Chaos Creation	The world of Cosmic Creation
creatio ex nihilo – creation out of nothing (the potential of a womb-like place).	*Ex nihilo nihil fit* – nothing comes from nothing therefore the void is an empty sterile place.
Order emerges from the void - chaos.	Order is created by Order - cosmos.
Cycles - order returns to chaos, chaos produces order.	Evolution – order never returns to chaos or its own previous position.
All things are linked in a web of relationships.	All things are separate.
Divinity is polymorphic.	Divinity is in human form.
The world is co-created in an emergent manner without hierarchies.	Order creates the world for the use of humans
Pluralism – many voices. All are equal.	Monism – one voice. A hierarchal system.
Events emerge as patterns – this leads to ritual and repetition as working tools.	Causal – every event is the result of earlier, logical action - this leads to experimentation and reductionism.
Astrology, omens and superstitions - the non-linear world.	Science - the linear world.

Figure 4 – a comparison of the two world views of chaos and cosmos

2
THE WAR OF THE WORLDS

The place outside the walled garden of order is a place with no name. It is a vilified and cursed place which has been denied a voice by the new world view of cosmos. However, this place of no name has not withered and disappeared. Instead it has crept into our culture in a million little ways: sometimes as a fairy story that speaks of the danger of the wild woods, the place beyond the village; at other times in our historical references when we speak of the "ordered" world of the Romans and the "chaotic" world of the Barbarians. We acknowledge its presence by showing our bias when we define ugly as a lack symmetry and think of events of serendipities and superstition, or any form of divination, as so called foolish practices. This place of no name is alive and well, we are just not meant to see it or speak of it.

The beginning of this denial may well lie in the Baby-lonian creation myth of the *Enuma Elish* which unlike creation myths of the east, rages with bloodshed, plots, betrayals and finally a mother set against a great-grandson. The myth-makers of the *Enuma Elish* dreaded the intention-filled nothingness, personified as the dragon Tiamat and described her as "The chaos of Tiamat was the mother of them all"[1]. For this is myth conceived by humans who lived in terror of the loss of order. A myth probably created at a time when a culture sought to justify its paranoid actions of murder and massacre.

The narrative begins, as we saw in the previous chapter with Tiamat defending her children against a "terrible" father. However, once her sons turn on their father and use spells to

---

[1] R.Abraham. *Chaos, Gaia, Eros*:128.

murder him in his sleep, Tiamat becomes enraged and seeks revenge against her patricidal children. She is nearly victorious and her sons contemplate peace by asking for mercy but their great fear of Tiamat stops them. Instead they approach Marduk, Tiamat's great grandson and a child born of the sun. Golden and sparkling in the clear sunlight, he is probably our oldest mythic hero, and in the realm of a true hero the handsome Marduk brings hope and joy to all who look upon him.

> Alluring was his figure, sparkling the lift of his eyes.
> Lordly was his gait, commanding from of old.
> When Ea saw him, the father who begot him,
> He exulted and glowed, his heart filled with gladness[2].

Marduk pursues Tiamat mounted in his war chariot and, armed with new weapons, he rides out to face her:

> He harnessed and yoked to it a team-of-four,
> The Killer, the Relentless, the Trampler, the Swift.
> Their lips were parted, their teeth bore poison.
> They were tireless and skilled in destruction.
> On his right he posted the Smiter[3], fearsome in battle,
> On the left the Combat, which repels all the zealous.
> For a cloak he was wrapped in an armor of terror;
> With his fearsome halo his head was turbaned.
> The lord went forth and followed his course,
> Towards the raging Tiamat he set his face[4].

But Marduk does not use his weapon *Smiter*. Instead he splits Tiamat in two using only the four winds and a net, for one cannot stab or cut the void. A part of Tiamat he leaves in the earth; the other he places above the earth and makes the

---

[2] L.W. King : Tablet I line 89-90.
[3] Possibly a sword.
[4] ibid, Tablet IV line 51 – 60.

covering of the heavens.[5] His mission completed, Marduk settles down to rule his kingdom. Yet, even as the supreme god, Marduk knows that his great grandmother was Tiamat, the intention-filled nothingness from which he and his kin have been created. He may be the supreme ruler, "Firm in his order, his command unalterable, the utterance of his mouth no god shall change"[6] but he is not alone, not the only god.

This battle of Marduk against the chaotic dragon Tiamat was carried into the myth's re-write a thousand or so years later in Revelations (12:7-9), as the battle between the archangel Michael and the archangel Lucifer – Satan:

> And there was war in heaven: Michael and his
> angels fought against the dragon; and the dragon
> fought his angels. And prevailed not; neither was
> their place found any more in heaven. And the great
> dragon was cast out, that old serpent, called the
> Devil and Satan, which deceiveth the whole world:
> he was cast out into the earth, and his angels were
> cast out with him[7].

In this version of the myth, the archangel Michael plays the role of Marduk but the dragon is no longer the mighty and worthy creative force of Tiamat. The dragon is reduced to an asexual evil beast and eventually morphs into the dragon killed by St. George in the 4th century story of Christian victory over pagan religions.

The story has also followed us into the modern era, with its most known version told in Ridley Scott's film *Alien* (1979), a modern box-office success now of cult standing. In the film the evil female monster of chaos is in conflict with a female of the realm of cosmos, played by Sigourney Weaver. Both are

---

[5] R.Abraham *Chaos, Gaia, Eros*:129.
[6] L.W. King. tablet VII lines 151 – 152.
[7] Roy Chamberlin and Herman Feldman.(1950).*The Dartmouth Bible*. Boston, USA: Houghton Mifflin.

locked in mortal combat. The famous female monster wants to breed with the human race and therefore, from cosmos' point of view, to potentially destroy all of humanity. This fertile, saliva-dripping, scaly, female monster is a version of Tiamat and, at least in this story, she is once again female and fertile. Nevertheless Weaver's task in Scott's film, like that of Marduk's, St. Michael's and St. George's is not to negotiate with the monster but to totally eliminate her. With its chaotic symbolism the dragon reflects all that is negative and destructive and has to be condemned, overthrown, damned, killed, beheaded and eliminated for all time. These are not battles in which resolution or compromise can be considered. They demand total victory and total eradication of all that belongs to the dragon.

Granted, there is a natural polarity between the philosophies of chaos and cosmos. The opening four lines of *Genesis* informs us it is the polarity of the day and the night, that which is clear and that which is unclear, that which is complex versus that which is simple, the conscious state of being awake versus the unconscious state of being asleep. However, unlike the gentle Chinese figure of Pangu or the non-threatening figures of the Dreamtime, the Ungambikula, in the *Enuma Elish* the tension between the polarities is a source of great conflict. In the *Enuma Elish*, one side of this pair, Order, wants to be a singleton.

As we have already discussed, cosmic thinking requires a causal logic, a linear simplicity and a series of events that can be used to build further knowledge. In contrast, chaos thinking is based in seemingly non-causal links between patterns reliant on repeating themes with no regard to size, time, or nature. In Eastern philosophy these differences are allowed to stand side by side. Non-causal based systems such as the *I-Ching, Feng Shui* and the philosophy of acupuncture are not vilified, for their creation myths do not have this conflict. However, to the Western mind, forged from a creation myth of strife, these differences are a threatening anathema to the order of cosmos. Indeed in the West these two philosophies of chaos and cosmos have been locked in battle for several thousand years[8]. It has also been argued that this battle is the driving force behind the missionary zeal of Christians in their desire to rid the world of chaos by the conversion of the primitive or evil savage[9], an argument which links Marduk and order with monotheism and the dragon of Tiamat with plurality and paganism.

In the West therefore it was, and still is today, important for the self appointed protectors of Order - the Marduks, the St. Michaels and the St. Georges - to attack any artefact of the chaotic paradigm in Western culture. Such crusaders unconsciously take the role of Marduk and seek artefacts such as omens, superstition and astrology and dedicate their lives to Tiamat's total and utter extinction. For these crusaders who stand on the front-line guarding Order, anything which dares to even suggest that there is a place outside the walled garden has to be eliminated, whether these suggestions are ideas and/ or people.

Yet, despite the vigilance of these crusaders, I slowly came to realise that my family, like so many other people, only pretended to live inside the walled garden but in reality they actually lived outside the walls, in the world of chaos. Indeed many people give lip service to the world of cosmos but they too live their lives outside the garden hoping that no one will notice, in many cases not even noticing themselves. Indeed if you believe in any form of synchronicity or see any meaning in random events, then a part of you is living in a world which

[8] see R.Abraham. *Chaos, Gaia, Eros.*
[9] M.Butz. *Chaos and Complexity – Implications for Psychological Theory and Practice*: 214.

is not meant to exist. A part of you has a foot in the place with no name.

But how did the walled garden come into existence, and why are the walls so high and why are those people who leave its manicured borders of causal flower beds so vilified?

How Cosmos won the West - the early years

Marduk's victory within the Western mind was neither fast nor was it easy. The story stretches from the philosopher Heraclitus (540 – 480 B.C.E.) to the work of Charles Darwin (1809-1882) and is littered with casualties, mostly on the chaotic side of the battle.

The creative force hidden in the darkness deep in the turbulence of chaos was a theme central to the philosophy of Heraclitus when he proposed a law which he called *logos*, where forces moved towards each other. Only fragments of his work remain but he states:

> What is opposite strives towards union, out of the diverse there arises the most beautiful harmony, and the struggle makes everything come about in this way[10].

Heraclitus stated that if everything was in a state of flux, then everything was constantly changing and if everything was changing, then nothing could be known. As Heraclitus says, "All is flux, nothing stays still"[11]. Chaos, argued Heraclitus, does not allow for the concept of knowledge and his most famous statement is that we cannot step into the same river twice as the water has moved on. We can, therefore, never know the river as it is always changing.

---

[10] Requoted from Klaus Mainzer. (1994). *Thinking in Complexity: The complex dynamics of matter, mind and mankind.* London: Sringer-Verlag :17.
[11] Laertius, Diogenes. (2004). *Lives of Eminent Philosophers.* http://www.quotationspage.com/quote/24074.html   Accessed 15 September, 2004.

Heraclitus' philosophical terminus was not acceptable to the Greek mind in its pursuit of the clarity of knowledge. Parmenides of Elea (ca 500 B.C.E.) presented a counter argument to Heraclitus. He suggested that the world was solid and uniform, without motion or time and that all apparent motion or change was an illusion. Plato (ca 427-347 B.C.E.) also answered Heraclitus by suggesting that chaos could exist in the land of the living, the sub-lunar world, but that the divine or godly world was perfect, orderly, totally stable and consistent. Plato talked of two worlds: the one above being perfect, stable and orderly and labelled as divine and the other below, being the sub-lunar world, where all things were subject to change. To the divine world he attributed knowledge, simplicity, elegance and truth[12] and since this time these characteristics have been linked to that world[13]. Plato's philosophy was a balance between the linear, logical world of order defined as divine, and the non-linear, inter-linked world of Heraclitus, defined as chaotic.

By seeing the world split into two, Plato had in fact mirrored the earlier actions of Marduk, for he, like Marduk placed one portion of the world in the sky and the other onto the earth. Plato may well have been the first person to seriously promote the idea of the two worlds existing side by side. But Plato, having had the genius to clearly see the two worlds of chaos and cosmos, made the mistake of attributing creation to the linear world, the world of order. In Plato's defence, unlike later thinkers, he did not actually deny the existence of the non-linear chaotic world, he merely cast it as non-divine and

---

[12] J.V Luce. (1992). *An Introduction to Greek Philosophy*. London: Thames and Hudson Ltd: 99.
[13] Bernard Williams. (2001). "Plato – The invention of philosophy", in Monk, Ray. Raphael, Frederic (eds). *The Great Philosophers*. London: Phoenix :88.

consequently in his philosophy, barren, whereas later generations were to deny Tiamat's very existence.

Plato also saw shape and geometry as one of the pure forms of knowledge and considered that there were only two forms of motion: the straight line and the curve. The curve, being the more perfect of motions because it could go on without end, was assigned to the divine imperishable element, the quintessence (5th element) which formed the unchanging celestial spheres and the stars. The straight line was assigned to the four elements and placed in the sub-lunar changing, imperfect world. Within Plato's divine unchanging perfect world the planets orbited the earth in perfect circles attached to perfect spheres.

However, there was one problem. The perfect planets would, from time to time, appear to travel backwards in the sky. Plato's approach to the observed retrograde motion of the planets was destined to have a profound impact on future research methods[14], for he assumed that one day this motion would be understood and it would comply with the divine circular motion (*Timaeus*). He did not ponder why the planets moved in a retrograde manner, rather he assumed that the explanation would fit into his perfect model. In this way he laid down the philosophical foundation for all acceptable answers. From this point onwards truth could only be truth if it was ordered and regular. It was Apollonius of Perga (ca 210 B.C.E.) who eventually fully fulfilled Plato's expectation by refining the idea that the planetary orbits contained epicycles: smaller perfect circles located at points on bigger perfect circles.

Plato's abandonment of the sub-lunar world left no place for a philosophical commentary on life itself. To enable some

---

[14] K.Mainzer. *Thinking in Complexity: The complex dynamics of matter, mind and mankind:* 24-26.

[15] J.V.Luce. *An Introduction to Greek Philosophy:* 116.

enquiry into the sub-lunar world, Aristotle (384-322 BCE), Plato's student, introduced the ideas of form and matter. Form was that which made the substance what it was and matter was the substance that had been shaped by the form[15]. Matter had the *potential* to be formed but it was not until matter has been formed that reality came into being. Wood was wood but it was the principle of *form* which made it a tree or a table. Aristotle believed the physical realm contained perfection and concluded that despite always being in flux, it moves towards specific ends, demonstrating a certain teleology (*telos* = 'end' or 'purpose'). The essence of a thing, he argued, did not lie outside the physical realm but was contained within it. In this model matter is the irregular mass but has an awareness of its final and perfect form. Like an acorn dreaming to be an oak tree, the acorn contained within itself a teleological property, a force which pulled it towards becoming an oak tree rather than a stalk of wheat.

For Aristotle, this movement towards the perfect form and the resulting changes through which matter passed was the key to understanding the living world. He believed that matter yearned for its own perfection. The brilliance of Aristotle was to recognise this now-acknowledged major principal of living systems[16] - that matter seeks its own order and that there are patterns which have their own 'desire' to unfold in certain ways. Aristotle's concept of teleology actually belongs in Tiamat's world of self-ordering and emerging patterns. For teleology is a pulling towards an end which is *not* known in contrast to order's causal force as a pushing agent towards an end which *is* predictable. Western thinking embraced the work of Aristotle but having already silenced

---

[16] Stuart Kauffman.(1995). *At Home in the Universe: The Search for the Laws of Self-Organization and Complexity*. New York: Oxford University Press: 24,25.

Tiamat, chose to forget his teachings on teleology[17]. For the Greeks there was no intellectual space for teleology and thus it was allocated to religion – God planned everything and is pulling us towards Him, a perfect divine state.

Later thinkers blended Aristotle's work, minus his idea of *telos*, with Plato's thinking of the divine world of knowledge and perfection to produce a philosophy that could be applied to all research into the workings of the sub-lunar world. With knowledge equated to elegance, one could only seek solutions in the sub-lunar realm if they were also elegant even if this was at the expense of the observed facts. Truth, defined as logical predictability, and the divine were seen as inseparable[18]. If an inelegant answer persisted, then that answer did not exist, an attitude with which the Italian mathematician, Galileo Galilei (1564-1642) was destined to do battle.

But ninety years before Galileo, when Nicolaus Copernicus (1473-1543) looked for a solution to the observable irregularities in the movement of the solar system, he fitted his solution into Plato's framework. Working within Plato's original question of an elegant solution, he placed the sun in the centre of the solar system and allowed the earth to orbit on one of its perfect circles and thereby explained the retrograde motion of the planets in a simpler fashion: "Copernicus considered that greater simplicity in the sense of 'natural' circular motion to be a sign of proximity to reality. …"[19] Simplicity was not only understood as the demand for

---

[17] Anthony Mansueto.(1998). "Cosmic Teleology and the Crisis of the Sciences", in *Philosophy of Science*. on-line Journal of papers presented for the Twentieth World Congress of Philosophy, in Boston, Massachusetts 10 August, 1998. http://www.bu.edu/wcp/Papers/Scie/ScieMans.htm Accessed 16 October, 2004.

[18] Ilya Prigogine and Isabelle Stengers.(1984). *Order Out of Chaos: Man's New Dialogue with Nature*. New York: Bantam Books : 7.

[19] K. Mainzer. *Thinking in Complexity: The complex dynamics of matter, mind and mankind*: 27,29.

an economical methodology; Copernicus saw it as one of the features of truth. Although completely comfortable within neo-Platonism, Copernicus' new model of the solar system began a one hundred year period of change where many different models of the solar system were proposed. The resultant upheaval provided the intellectual space for the work of Johannes Kepler (1571-1630) and Galileo Galilei - two men whose work was to rearrange the domains of cosmos and chaos.

The domination of the cosmic paradigm

The supernova of 1604, observed by Kepler and presented in his work titled *De Stella Nova* published in Prague (1606), was more than just an interesting observation in astronomy. It was the unmistakably-blinding, undeniably-obvious raw evidence of a change in the perfect unchangeable divine realm – the sky had changed. Earlier in his *Mysterium cosmographicum* (published in Tübingen, 1596), Kepler had pursued Plato's thinking with regard to perfect shapes and created his model of the solar system which based planetary distance on regular solids. However, his later work, *Astronomia Nova* published in 1609 after his discovery of the supernova, was the demise of the Platonic concepts of simplicity. In this work Kepler produced his first two laws of planetary motion. The first law stated that the planets move in ellipses with the sun at one focus of the ellipse; the second law stated that the arc described by the orbiting planet describes equal area in equal time, and since the paths were elliptical, that law showed that the planets had to be irregular in their speed as they orbited the sun. Kepler's laws removed the perfect circles from the divine realm and, combined with his observation of the supernova of 1604, the sky became a place of change which could therefore no longer contain the divine. With Kepler shaking apart the divine sky, a challenge also occurred to Plato's idea that one could never gain measurable, predictable knowledge of the sub-lunar world.

Galileo was a contemporary of Kepler and also interested in motion but Galileo was interested in motion in the sub-lunar world and he proceeded to formulate laws which explained and predicted some of the workings of this un-divine place. Galileo showed that the world of "no order" had order. His approach to the sub-lunar world was so radical that the French philosopher Rene Descartes (1596-1650) rejected Galileo's physics totally because he, Galileo, in investigating the cause of motion or heaviness, had simply measured it.[20] Kepler and Galileo corresponded with each other but both pursued their own endeavours: one the motion of the heavens; the other, motion in the sub-lunar world. Nevertheless the combined impact of their work was to swap the polarity of cosmos and chaos. Through the publications of Kepler, order fell from the sky but through the work of Galileo it found a home in the sub-lunar world. For a short and fearful time the sky was once again ruled by chaos.

It is hard for us in our present day lives to understand the upheaval this change in thinking would have produced. The still, perfect, divine sky suddenly became full of change and irregularity, shaking the very idea of God. This turbulent time is well-captured in the famous poem of John Donne written in 1611, *The First Anniversary*:

> And new Philosophy calls all in doubt,
> The Element of fire is quite put out;
> The sun is lost, and th'earth, and no man's wit
> Can well direct him, where to look for it.
> And freely men confess, that this world's spent,
> When in the Planets, and the Firmament
> They seek so many new; they see that this
> Is crumbled out again to his Atomis.
> 'Tis all in pieces, all coherence gone;

---

[20] Drake Stillman. (1996). *Galileo*. Oxford UK: Oxford University Press:11.

> All just supply, and all relation:
> Princes, subject, father, son, are things forgot...

The perfect, divine, celestial sphere was no longer ruled by the divine. Now anything could happen. This point is summarised by Kepler in a letter that he wrote to Herwart von Hohenzollern, the Catholic Chancellor of Bavaria, in 1609 where he talks of a need to return order once again to the heavens but under new rules:

> My aim is to show that the heavenly machine is not
> a kind of divine, live being, but a kind of clockwork,
> insofar as nearly all the manifold motions are caused
> by a most simple, magnetic, and material force, just
> as all motions of the clock are caused by a simple
> weight. And I also show how these physical causes
> are to be given numerical and geometrical
> expression[21].

By 1619 Kepler had published his third law of planetary motion in *Harmonices mundi libri* V (Linz) in which he showed there existed an "elegant" relationship between the orbital period of a planet and its distance from the sun. The movement of the planets was thus explained in three clear laws and thus the surety of simplicity and elegant order, although somewhat revised, was returned to the sky.

Cosmos now ruled both earth and the sky. The work of Galileo gave predictable order to the realm of the earth and the work of Kepler enabled the divine sky to become the divine machine. The complex, inter-related world of life had to this point been ignored and classified as unknowable, now had its very existence denied. Tiamat was not only defeated but her presence was surgically removed from the equation.

---

[21] Re-quoted from Arthur Koestler. (1959). *The Sleepwalkers. A History of Man's Changing Vision of the Universe.* Harmondsworth, UK: Penguin Books Ltd :345.

It was Isaac Newton (1643-1727) who delivered the final great blow to Tiamat. His discovery of gravity, which seemed to explain the workings of the solar system, and his work in mathematics, which gave tools for working with shifting variables (calculus and differential equations), implied that the sub-lunar world could also be reduced to a machine where all things could eventually be predicted. Such clarity in the sub-lunar world left no place for a dragon named Tiamat; any fragments of belief which came from the world of the creative void was labelled as belonging either to the primitive world of "savages" or the foolish minds of the ignorant.

Newton bequeathed to us the Newtonian mechanical world made up of a mechanical sky and a mechanical earth. From this time forward Newtonian science considered that all things could be known and all things could be predicted. The Newtonian scientific quest, forgetting that chaos ever existed, was to have nothing but order[22]. This was summarised by Pierre Simon de Laplace (1749-1827), the French mathematician and astronomer, who described the position of this new found quest of science in what is now called Laplace's Demon:

> We may regard the present state of the universe as the effect of its past and the cause of its future. An intellect which at any given moment knew all of the forces that animate nature and the mutual positions of the beings that compose it, if this intellect were vast enough to submit the data to analysis, could condense into a single formula the movement of the greatest bodies of the universe and that of the lightest atom; for such an intellect nothing could be uncertain and the future just like the past would be present before its eyes[23].

---

[22] Fritjof Capra. (1996). *The Web of Life: A New Scientific Understanding of Living Systems*. New York: Doubleday :119.
[23] Roger Hahn. (2005). *Pierre Simon Laplace 1749-1827: A Determined Scientist*. Cambridge, MA: Harvard University Press.

Yet before Newton died he unwittingly pulled at the thread of undoing of this supreme rulership of cosmos. For Newton was unable to predict the exact position of three orbiting planets, all influencing each other with the force of gravity. Newton's unsolvable dilemma became known as the Three-Body Problem and set a challenge for generations of mathematicians. The eventual solution would take until the early 20th century to solve and open another chapter in this long battle.

Meanwhile by suggesting that an organism was not a machine, Immanual Kant (1724-1804) disagreed with Newton's mechanical, knowable, ordered world[24]. Sensing the silenced presence of the void, Kant reasoned that life was different to the realm of separate objects and that it belonged to another world, another set of ideas and principles. However, Charles Darwin (1809-1882) ended that debate. His theory of evolution which suggested that complex organisms could evolve purely by the pressure of survival of the fittest removed any teleological or natural self-organising elements from the argument and was held as the final proof of the validity of the reductionist, mechanised world view. Thus life was based on chance and became mechanical.[25] Existence was nothing more than the by-product of genes driven by the force of evolution and fuelled by the need for survival.

Marduk claimed the crown by using this new weapon of Darwinism. Now he could rule in peace. Marduk, the solar king of light, the supreme god of Order, had dominion over all things, those above and what was below. Tiamat was dead.

---

[24] I. Kant. (1971). *Kritik der Urteilskraft.* Ed. G Lehmann. Stuttgart: Reclam:340.
[25] S.Kauffman. *At Home in the Universe: The Search for the Laws of Self-Organization and Complexity*: 6.

Astrology placed in an intellectual ghetto

But Tiamat refused to die. Ignored and denied any form of voice, the chaotic world now lived in an intellectual ghetto, developing a ghetto language and a ghetto culture. Newtonian science now labelled any evidence of spontaneous order emerging from the creative void as foolish superstition or simply coincidences. Intuitions were at best odd feelings; at worst associated with evil. Stories of repeating links between events became "old wives tales" and supporters, believers or even those who sought to understand or even acknowledge the possible interlinking patterns of life were considered cranks, charlatans, swindlers or devil worshippers. This was the ghetto outside the walled garden.

Many astrologers have pushed against the social and intellectual ostracism of this ghetto and have sought to find a home for astrology within the safety of the walled garden. Motivated by the desire for membership of the world view of cosmos, some researchers fully believe that astrology belongs in the world of cause and effect; other researchers unaware of the other world of chaos, have striven in this endeavour thinking that there is only the world of the walled garden.

The Astrological Reformers – the long hard road of failure

Claudius Ptolemy (ca 150 C.E.), thought to be the single most influential astrologer/astronomer in the history of the subject[26], and standing on the shoulders of seven hundred years of Greek philosophy, turned his attention to the physics of the day, astrology. Greek horoscopic astrology had emerged in the 4th century B.C.E.; five centuries later Ptolemy, within the Platonic tradition, strove to correct, improve, and perfect the logic of the subject. He changed the term rulers, eliminated

---

[26] J.Tester. A History of Western Astrology: 3.

one of the triplicity rulers and generally debated the philosophical logic of astrology. Ptolemy's apparent desire was to reconcile astrology with the new glorification of order. His aim was to build a logical Aristotelian foundation for astrology in the same way as he had laid the foundations of astronomy in his *Almagest* (The Great Work). Ptolemy's work had a large impact on the practice of astrology but did little to allow the discipline of astrology entry to the world of cosmos.

A thousand years later another scientific reforming astrologer, Spanish theologian Ramon Lull (1232 – 1316), also tried to develop a "scientific" or more orderly astrology. He deconstructed all of the astrological components of a horoscope to their simplest form, assigned them a letter and then rebuilt them into a form of algebra in the pursuit of gaining a consistent understanding of astrological patterns. This reductionist approach of seeing astrology as a linear system[27] was not carried forward by future astrologers, nor did it give the discipline of astrology entry to the world of cosmos. Ramon Lull died a martyr while seeking to convert the Saracens to the Christian faith. However, the mere fact that Lull had attempted to bring astrology into the world of order was sufficient evidence of "evil practices" to deny him beatification by the Catholic Church.

Some three hundred years later Johannes Kepler, seeking a mechanical sky, reformed the art of aspecting in astrology. Prior to Kepler, the importance of the geometrical relationship between planets was not only contained in their ecliptical distances but was also dependant on the planet's "personality" and "place of residence"[28] Certain "places of residence" did not have easy communication with other places and certain

---

[27] Ramon Lull. (1994). *Treatise on Astronomy*. Translator Shapar, Kris. (editor) Hand, Robert. Berkley Springs, USA. Golden Hind Press: v.

[28] Masha'allah. (1998). *On Reception*. Translator Hand, Robert. USA: Arhat Publications: 2.

planets did not have characteristics that matched or responded to other planets. Furthermore, a planet related to other planets in two ways, firstly, with its own orb of influences, (aspecting by moiety), and secondly by being duty bound to any planet in its own household (reception). These two relationships effectively meant that the planets functioned like members of a small community, the village of the horoscope. Within this idea of a horoscopic village some planets would have a greater influence than others. If a planet was the "guest" of such an influential planet, then it received that planet's hospitality and could function more effectively in the horoscope. If a planet was not the guest of the influential planet but was within that influential planet's orb (in aspect), then the planet also gained from that relationship. The chart was a village of planets all engaged in relationships and populated with rulers, paupers, rich merchants, land-lords, tenants, honoured guests, foreigners, and so forth.

Fuelled by his desire for a mechanical world Kepler removed the "people" from the horoscope and replaced them with mechanical aspecting. His aspecting theory implied that if a person enters a room, their relationship to the group of people in that room will be dependant only on their geometrical relationship to each of them. Their history with the group, their personality, appearance, culture and body language will have nothing to add to their ability to form relationships with any member of that group. Kepler, freed of the confines of the relationships needs within a horoscope, could then add more aspects to the astrological lore - the semi-sextile, semi-square, sesquiquadrate and quincunx – and effectively turned the planets from "people" into orbiting rocks. Kepler cleared from astrology what he considered to be indefinable and unmanageable components – the village of the chart - for him, geometry and number was all there was. Kepler's reforms did have a substantial impact on the philosophy of Western astrology, as it changed the nature or the role of the planets in a chart but his work had no impact on astrology gaining membership to the world of cosmos.

Geometry was also the quest of the 20th century German astrologer, Reinhold Ebertin (1901-1988). He developed what he called cosmobiology which utilises planetary midpoints and their resulting geometrical "trees". In producing these midpoint trees Ebertin totally removed the meanings of zodiac signs, aspects and houses from astrology, stripping them down even further to their bare planetary geometrical patterns. This was Ebertin's attempt to create scientific astrology and set it apart from what he saw as being its more ancient, imperfect and vulgar origins. As he says:

> Cosmobiology has, through the work of the author
> of this book, become increasingly well-known
> within the last forty years from those aspects mark-
> ing it off from ancient astrology[29].

It is, in effect, an extension of Ptolemy's, Lull's and Kepler's drive to reduce astrology down to simpler, more orderly units to which one can then apply reductionist thinking. Although his work has had an impact on the practice of astrology, it has still not permitted the discipline of astrology to gain entry to the world of cosmos.

This quest for acceptance into the causal world of logical order was also reflected in the work of Michel and Francoise Gauquelin. While not attempting to reform astrology, the Gauquelins were seeking to prove astrology within the scientific model. Their most famous research result, *L'Influence des Astres* (the Mars Effect), was published in 1955. In this research the Gauquelins showed that the tendency of the diurnal position of Mars to be in particular zones of the natal horoscopes of French sports champions was statistically

---

[29] Reinhold Ebertin. (1940). *The Combination of Stellar Influences.* Tempe, USA: AFA :11.

significant. What followed was over forty years of turmoil between astrological skeptics and the Gauquelins. The Mars Effect is still considered by some to be a valid statistical result, yet regardless of whether this can be seen as proof of astrology or not, it is not the type of proof that most astrologers desire, as it does nothing to justify their daily practice of astrology.[30]

Astrology seeks acceptance as a Sacred Science

There are, however, other ways of seeking membership into the cosmic paradigm. Just as one can seek cosmic membership through a display of repeatable linearity in the sub-lunar world, one can also seek this membership in the divine world.

There are many who, over the last two thousand years, have reasoned that astrology was far richer than just quantity and number and they have, in effect, placed astrology into the divine realm. Astrology, for this group, is a form of sacred science, a type of spiritual knowledge whose practice leads to a deeper understanding of the mystery of life and its relationship to the divine. This is actually the divine quest of Plato's cosmic world view and as such its definition and nature has been reworked by many thinkers. One such philosopher was Plotinus (204-270) who raised intellectual contemplation to a mystical principle, creating what is now known as neo-Platonism.

Briefly, Plotinus considered the idea of the human soul and taught that it was composed of a higher and a lower part. The higher part of the soul was unchangeable and divine and provided the lower part with life, while the lower part was the seat of the personality and therefore full of all the passions and vices of life. It was the duty of the lower part of the soul to ascend, through intellectual pursuit, to form a union with its higher part. Neo-Platonism has been defined as "the

---

[30] G.Phillipson. *Astrology in the Year Zero*:144.

intellectualists reply to the ... yearning for personal salvation".[31] We can take this one step further and suggest that neo-Platonism is Order seeking its own salvation exclusively through its own specifications of intellect and knowledge.

This was a powerful idea for the new paradigm of cosmos and St. Augustine of Hippo (354 – 430) took the neo-Platonist philosophy of Plotinus and poured it into the heart of the new religion, Christianity. The two modes of thinking were highly compatible. The divine realm of neo-Platonism could be ruled by Christ the One, whose divine monism automatically produced Plato's concept of the divine realm. It was a marriage literally made in heaven. Thus with the new religion of Christianity elegantly personalised in neo-Platonism, a person who desired a higher purpose to life could take the pathway of seeking knowledge. Knowledge became the pathway to God. In this way the linear world of Order could not only provide the mechanism for the discovery of new knowledge but it also suggested that this knowledge would actually lead to personal salvation. Such a salvation leads to a divine being who is defined as external, existing outside the system, a transcendent God.

This is a powerful and seductive philosophy and it does offer a shelter for astrologers fleeing from the dryness of science. Yet comforting as it may be for some practitioners to claim a place for astrology in the ways of neo-Platonism, such a philosophical framework is still limited and defined by the victorious Marduk and his resulting cosmos and its glorification of order. For to see astrology as a pathway upon which a person can move closer to the union with their own personal *higher* soul is to still seek membership of the cosmic paradigm via the loophole of spirituality.

---

[31] Frederick S.J.Copleston. (1962). A *History of Philosophy* (vol. I, part II): *Greece and Rome*. New York, USA: Image Books: 216.

Astrology may well be a form of spirituality but if it is, then according to chaotic myths its concept of divinity is immanent rather then transcendent (within rather than without), and pluralistic. It is a divine which is polymorphic, favours no one species and no one object, and is constantly moving within all things. It is a non-planning, non-personal form of divinity without any hierarchical structure and definitely not the form of divine envisaged by St. Augustine when he blended neo-Platonism with Christianity.

Life in the Ghetto

The impact of living in a world defined by the philosophy of cosmos means that astrologers are ambivalent about their identity and their purpose. A study by Phillipson[32] on this subject shows that amongst the different groups of astrologers there are those who believe that astrology is a science and this group continues to pursue research using the scientific method. Phillipson also notes astrologers who link astrology to a form of magic and practise their craft closer to divination, while another group see astrology as a language. Still another approach is found in the work of Patrick Curry who considers the practise of astrology to be an instrument of enchantment, a way in which humanity encounters mystery, awe and wonder.[33] His focus is that it is necessary for astrology to be marginalised by mainstream thought in order for it to maintain this position. Indeed in the same passage Curry notes that any success gained by astrology in becoming mainstream "would be at the price of its soul."

Astrology may be all of these things – scientific, magical, a language or a vehicle of enchantment – or it may be none of them. However, with its confusion of identity, diverse

---

[32] see G.Phillipson. *Astrology in the Year Zero*.
[33] Roy Willis, Patrick Curry. (2004). *Astrology Science and Culture, Pulling down the moon*. New York: Berg : 89.

communities and many different forms and definitions, it just may be demonstrating its inability to find a place to stand within the cosmic philosophy. Indeed, it has been trying to find a place in cosmic philosophy since that philosophy began but has continually failed to do so.

So astrology, damned by the establishment and ill-defined by its multiplicity of expressions, may need to be re-appraised. Instead of its followers and its critics remaining stuck in a polarised argument between the spiritual versus scientific, both of which are roles within the cosmic paradigm, we may be able to break out of this deadlock by considering it to be part of chaos philosophy, a child of Tiamat the dragon.

For if astrology has been born at the time of dragons, looks like a dragon, performs like a dragon and is treated like a dragon, maybe it is a dragon.

3

CHAOS FOR BEGINNERS – THE STIRRING OF TIAMAT

It was late at night and Edward was tired. All he wanted to do was close up the lab and drive the twenty miles back home but he knew he could get one more run done before he called it a night. The year was 1961 and Edward, a meteorologist at the Massachusetts Institute of Technology, was attempting to use computers to model the weather. The economic potential was inestimable, for if one could predict the weather, then one could learn how to make the right weather happen when one wanted it and he, Edward Lorenz, like any other scientist, was confident that empowered with the new tools of computing, the weather could become predictable[1].

Lorenz' computer weather model, named *Royal McBee*, was attempting to link a set of very precise parameters with every conceivable weather variable. But this night Lorenz was tired and it was late. He decided to shorten this last computer run by cutting in midway and hand entering the correct variables. His computer printouts of previous runs had given him the variables to an accuracy of three decimal places (thousandths) but the computer actually stored them with an accuracy of six decimal places (millionths). So unintentionally rounding them off, Lorenz hand entered the variables to only three decimal places. He set his computer running and went to make himself a coffee.

When Lorenz returned he found that rather than showing the expected weather system, *Royal McBee* was instead producing totally different patterns. He later discovered that the absence

---

[1] James Gleick. (1987). *Chaos: making a new science.* New York: Viking-Penguin: 65-69.

of those tiny missing decimal places had caused havoc in his system and that the smallest changes in his initial starting values had produced extremely different weather patterns. More alarming was the fact that these effects were not linear. He could not, for example, control the size of a tornado by pushing a variable one way or the other. A slight nudge of the tornado-producing variable would flip the weather into sunny calm seas or burning heat. His weather model was not functioning in a predictable or logical manner.

Lorenz had modelled the biosphere as best he could and in his attempt to mirror this richly-interlinked, variant dependant and sensitive environment he had unknowingly computer-modelled something else. Lorenz had done his job too well; his computerized biosphere had started to act like the real biosphere. Now Lorenz was not expecting to discover a new world, for since the time of Newton people had thought of the universe like a machine. What Lorenz had accidentally found was something else: a non-mechanical world with different rules and different properties. With the new tool of the computer, Lorenz had unknowingly created an elementary void, potentially the same creative void to which mythology referred. In these myths the void is a place filled with potential in which new patterns or order will spontaneously emerge. Little else is known about the void except that once new order emerges it will eventually return, emerge and return, time after time. In these myths, the first clear pattern is portrayed as the first independent life force which then helps to pull other forms out of the void. But that night Lorenz knew nothing of this void, for the void had long ago been denied an existence.

The Void – not as empty as cosmos thought
What Lorenz found was something that we already instinctually understand. It is simple but it was not expected to be found in

closed systems (those where all the variables are known) of numbers and computer programs. What we know is that if you put a group of strangers into a room together, then groups will form, conversations will occur, ideas will emerge, friendships will take shape, alliances will be forged, arguments will erupt, and romance may blossom. The list is endless. We also know that the precise nature of these events is unpredictable and if we put the same group of people in the same room a second time, there will be different conversations and different ideas. This is empirical knowledge which we take for granted and do not need scientific proof for assurance.

What Lorenz discovered that night was that this known spontaneous and unpredictable emergence of order belonged not only to the world of the living – people in a room, bees in a hive, fish in the sea - but was also a feature of the non-living such as weather patterns created by the interlinked components of the biosphere. Indeed all that was needed was that the "objects" be a part of a relationship-rich feedback environment: push one thing that pulls another that pushes back which then alters the first that in turn affects a third which tugs on the second and also a fourth – and so on. Whether this is a group of people in a room talking or a flock of birds flying or a collection of interlinked, networked variables, all of these relationship-rich groups will spontaneously produce new order which is not imagined and created by an external hand. This is order created with no artisan, order with no designer, *creatio ex nihilo* – creation out of nothing.

We all experience this spontaneous order as a part of our life. Every group we enter, whether for work or play gives rise to us wondering at the potential new patterns – friendships, hostilities, opportunities – that may form. Will these unpredictable patterns be good or will they be bad? Will this be a good group from which we will gain enjoyment or will it be a disaster of conflict and competition? Our very expectation of the spontaneous emergence of some type of pattern or order from the group means that we already empirically understand some of the features of chaos theory and is, in itself, a proof of the existence of the activity of the chaotic paradigm in our lives.

Furthermore we know that in any group some of the friendships will dissolve away while others will last for many years, some ideas discussed will grow and take root while others will return to the void and disappear. This is the new order that emerges and returns, emerges and returns. This is the swirling silt of the Nile in the Egyptian creation myth. No one can predictive its exact outcome; what we can predict is that the silt will form patterns and that order will emerge.

Classical science, with its focus on the mechanical world and its mastery of the world of separate objects, had no understanding of this phenomenon. Indeed classical science dictates that if we had a room full of "people", after a period of time each person would be found sitting or standing at an equal distance from each other in a silent room. Furthermore, within the thinking of classical science, if you want conversation to occur, if you want any form of order to emerge, it must be consciously and externally created. Additionally, once you have an external architect creating order, then you can reproduce the same order in the room every time by introducing the same causal elements. This is the world of order, repeatable and predictable. Drop a topic for discussion into our room and you will get exactly the same conversation unfolding. Classical science would be correct in its predictions about this group of people if we left them in the room until they died, sealed the room and left the bodies long enough, for all the atoms of their decomposed bodies would eventually spread evenly around the room and thus behave in a mechanical manner.

What Lorenz discovered was that non-living objects or variables in a relationship-rich environment spontaneously formed new order and new patterns in the same manner as living units of a living system. His model was simple and closed, meaning that he was working with a defined set of variables, yet even with this closed system, by changing the numbers just a little and starting the model running halfway through, he had effectively dropped slightly different topics of conversations into his "room" and returned to find totally different "conversation" happening in his "group".

Lorenz decided to focus on this phenomenon of making one small change to a variable creating unpredictable results. In 1963, he presented a paper[2] on this work and eventually it became titled: "Predictability: Does the Flap of a Butterfly's Wings in Brazil set off a Tornado in Texas?" He had discovered what was later defined as Sensitive Dependant to Initial Conditions and this became reduced to its initials SDIC. What SDIC indicates is that the smallest change in a complex interrelated system at the beginning of a process gives rise to *dis*-proportional differences at the end. We know this to be so in our lives: a small event in that room full of people can spark totally different long-term outcomes. However, now it had been found in the province of numbers, numbers which were simply influencing each other in a non-linear manner. Tiamat was stirring.

In 1975 James Yorke called Lorenz' butterfly effect *chaos*. The term was used with all the negative cultural values that chaos and disorder has come to mean in the Western world but now chaos was showing some type of order which could be formulated and computerised.

---

[2] Edward Lorenz."Deterministic nonperiodic flow"in *Journal of Atmospheric Sciences*. Vol.20 : 130—141.

French mathematician Henri Poincare (1854-1912) could have warned them about this. In 1899 he solved a mathematical problem that had been around since the time of Isaac Newton. It was Newton's Three-Body Problem which posed the question of how to predict the exact position of three planets all influencing each other by gravity. Poincare mathematically proved that there was no solution, as the positions of the planets could only be estimated. In this seemingly simple statement Poincare had shown the limits of the mechanical world. He proved that if there were three or more objects which all influenced each other, then their resultant activity could not be predicted. Poincare's solution revealed that the world of proof, statistics and probabilities which belonged to the scientific method, reached its limit when three or more objects were combined in a feedback relationship. With this solution Poincare laid the intellectual foundation stone for the emergence of Quantum mechanics and Heisenberg's Uncertainty Principle (1927) and he has retrospectively been named the grandfather of chaos theory.

However, at the time when Lorenz' complex weather predicting computer model was being funded, no one was aware of or concerned with Poincare's discovery. Indeed Poincare's solution was largely ignored, even in his time, as it was unacceptable to thinkers within the philosophy of cosmos who preferred the clockwork, predictable, mechanical world. By 1960 this had not changed and so for meteorologists confident of the exclusive existence of the mechanical world and given enough time and money, weather was expected to be predictable and hopefully controllable.

Systems that are mechanical are known as linear dynamic systems: if the air temperature only had an influence on the air pressure which is turn only influenced the humidity content of the atmosphere, and so on in a direct causal linear manner weather patterns would have fitted into the cosmic paradigm. But weather belongs to what is now known as a non-linear dynamic system (also called a chaotic system) and as Lorenz was to discover, totally inaccessible to the reductionist linear methodology of classical science[3].

This was a jolt to the scientific world. Since the work of Rene Descartes in the seventeenth century 'truth' has been defined as that which could be tested, classical science had declared as *true* the knowledge gained about measurable, quantitative mechanical subjects such as how fast, how heavy, how high, how hot, and so on - and doubtful or potentially *untrue* all the knowledge that could not be weighted and measured – phenomenological knowledge. The scientific method was designed to test linear-dynamic systems and, since only linear dynamic systems could pass this scientific standard, then only linear dynamic systems were considered to yield truths. It is a simple security-seeking process: if you can't "weight it", then you can't test it; if you can't test it, then it is not *true*; if it is not *true*, then it is false; if it is false, then it does not exist, then we can all feel safe in the delusion that everything is understood and controlled. Only the mechanical linear world could be proved in the scientific model and so *only* the mechanical linear world existed. There was no world outside the garden wall.

The dominancy of the mechanical world also imposed its philosophy on social systems. Superior or healthy systems were those which exhibited stability, reliability and predictability. Balance was and is considered the superior position for economies[4] and, by extension, the idea of balance became the goal for organisations, political systems, populations, communities and even individual lives. Health

[3] I.Prigogine and I.Stengers. *Order Out of Chaos: Man's New Dialogue with Nature* :75.
[4] Mitchell Waldrop.(1992). *Complexity: The Emerging Science at the Edge of Order and Chaos.* New York: Touchstone:17.

care and medicine urged one to lead a balanced, steady and consistent life[5], to live life like a machine thus mirroring the findings of classical science in our lives. But are we machines? The work of Newton, Poincare, Lorenz and many others since then indicates that objects or variables that exist in a relationship-rich environment do not function like a machine. Instead they function chaotically, like the void of creation myths brimming with new ideas, with new order emerging and returning. The people in our imaginary room are a non-linear dynamic system functioning in a chaotic manner until they die after which the atoms of their bodies will act according to a linear dynamic system (mechanical).

Like Columbus in 1492, Lorenz had discovered a new world, one that had always been there but long-since forgotten or unknown. Lorenz had discovered a creative place, a place rich in relationships from which new order spontaneously emerged without design, without drafting. Lorenz had discovered the void.

Looking into the void - Fractals
Well before Lorenz' weather experiments, something odd had been found hiding in the numbers of simple formula. "Fractals" from the Latin *fractua* - to be irregular - were discovered by Gaston Julia (1893-1978) and developed and named by Benoit Mandelbrot in 1975. Although they are a closed system of known variables fractals still produce a simple type of number-void and can be used to observe how the void creates patterns and order.

You already know what a fractal looks like even if you have never encountered this term before. Look around you now. Fractals are the shapes of nature, the leaves on a plant,

[5] John van Eenwyk. (1997). *Archetypes and Strange Attractors*. Toronto, Canada: Inner City Books :43.

landscapes, clouds, the wrinkles on your skin and the cauliflower sitting in your fridge. They surround us and fill our view with repeating patterns and shapes and we reproduce them in our designs - the Oriental rug on the floor, the paisley print of the curtains and the patterns in the wallpaper. We are familiar with fractals; they are the shapes and forms used by nature as the basic building blocks of life and landscapes. But more than this, the simple mathematically created fractals can provide us with a window into the workings of the chaotic paradigm. Through the geometry of computer generated fractals, we can create and visually explore "simple voids" and begin to understand some of the ways in which the void functions.

Gaston Julia played with numbers. He found that if he fed the result of a simple piece of calculation back into the calculation and kept repeating this action, some interesting outcomes occurred. He further found that if you plotted the answer of each step on a graph, the results could be observed as an image. This process of feeding the answer of a calculation back into itself is known as iteration. Iteration in mathematics is like feedback in living systems only a little simpler, as the first results of a calculation are fed back into the same formula to produce a second result which in turn is fed back into the formula to produce another result, and so on. What Julia found, and which was later confirmed and expanded by Mandelbrot, was that the patterns in the resulting graphs resembled the patterns of nature (see figure 5). The numbers used in the formula are special numbers called imaginary numbers or complex numbers[6]. These numbers have the extra ability to carry not only quantity but also a type of quality through any calculations and what Julia's work showed was that when we

---

[6] Imaginary numbers are the solution to the square root of a negative number, I.E. the square root of -25 is impossible in our normal numbering system but in imaginary numbers it is -5 or 5i. A complex number is the combination of an imaginary number with a real number.

Figure 5 – A fractal. This is a graph created by plotting the results produced by the iteration of an equation many tens of thousands of times. The observed pattern has not been designed but has formed naturally via the feedback loop of iteration.

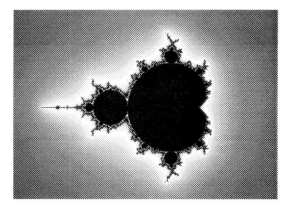

Figure 6 – The most famous fractal of all, known as the m-set, named after its discoverer Benoit Mandelbrot. This fractal is thought to contain all the shapes of nature.

use these quality/quantity numbers in a feedback loop, we are in fact creating a simple "void-like" environment.

The key point to grasp from this is that the patterns which emerged from the iteration of Julia's equations were not drafted by some external force; there was no artist, no designer, no mind considering what shape to produce next. The patterns spontaneously emerged as successive results were plotted on a graph. They are examples of *creatio ex nihilo* – creation out of nothing.

In expanding Julia's work, Mandelbrot discovered what is now known as the m-set (*see figure* 6). In looking at the m-set you can see the patterns emerging. The black area in the centre of the shape is where, as a result of iteration, the numbers have turned inward and slowly became stable at 0. The area outside the image is produced by numbers that, as a result of iteration, begin to move towards infinity, the speed at which they move towards infinity being coloured, in this example, as shades of grey. The actual shape itself is spontaneously created by the edge formed between the numbers that are turning inwards and the numbers that are starting to move into infinity. This edge, seen as a pattern, exists on what has been labelled as the "edge of chaos". Mandelbrot discovered the m-set when he was devising a method of computing all combinations of imaginary and real numbers which would "hover on this edge", and amazingly the m-set therefore contains all the possible shapes that nature or number can produce. It is in effect the mother board of all possible fractal shapes and in this way it is also considered the mother board of nature.

Self-Similarity and Scale Invariance – life's way of moving through time

Importantly Mandelbrot found that, in observing the visual patterns of fractals, that as they began to emerge, their unfoldment followed two consistent principles. These became known as scale invariance and self-similarity[7]. These two terms are firstly that a shape within an emerging pattern will reoccur at different magnitudes (scale invariance) and secondly, that each time it reoccurs, it is similar to but a little bit different from its previous expression (self-similarity). We can actually see these two principles at work when we zoom in to the edge of the m-set. We can see the repeating theme of the original image (*see figure 7*) but each time we see the m-set image it is a little different, slightly tilted or altered in some way. No matter how much we zoom in to the image we will continue to find new m-sets. The process goes on indefinitely.

Figure 7 – A magnification of the m-set in *figure 6*, showing the reproduction of the shape of the m-set reoccurring throughout the fractal. The level of magnification in the image above would mean that the first image in *figure 6* was now so large that it would stretch beyond the fixed star Sirius.

---

[7] Benoit Mandelbrot. (2004). "A geometry able to include mountains and clouds" in *The Colours of Infinity*. London, UK: Clear Books: 46-65.

Step back and take a breath.

The patterns you are seeing on paper are probably reflecting two of the great principles of life. You are looking at scale invariance, each m-set is thousands and even millions of times smaller than the original, yet you are also looking at the concept of self-similarity, each m-set is similar to the first but each is a little different, yet each tiny newly found m-set is complete and can be constantly magnified to find further m-sets.

Remember, this image has been spontaneously created with no architect and no graphic designer. It is a natural pattern formed from nothing more than a feedback process, yet once formed, the pattern keeps reproducing itself indefinitely with slight variations. We have focused on the recognisable m-set but there are also repeating spirals, twists and turns.

Although fractals are simplistic and a closed system, they do however allow us literally to see the way this *creatio ex nihilo* – creation out of nothing - actually works. For fractals not only allow us to look into the void which chaos creation myths suggest is the source of new patterns and order but we can also begin to see how these new patterns reproduce and emerge.

What other systems contain patterns like this? Think beyond the numbers and beyond the graphs. Living groups which by definition are involved in rich feedback loops also act like a fractal and spontaneously create patterns which reproduce over time through scale invariance and self-similarity[8]. These patterns can be seen in history as the rise and fall of civilizations, the repeating patterns of dictators, wars, discovery and renaissances. You can also see these patterns closer to home in your own family history and you will undoubtedly see these patterns in your own life.

---

[8] J.van Eenwyk. *Archetypes and Strange Attractors*: 65.

When I first went to Ireland, I like so many others who are the descendants of the Irish, decided to forage around in my family's old county and see what I could find. It had been over a hundred years since my great-grandfather had left Ireland and I had no contact with any living members of my current Irish relatives, however I was not looking for living people, I was looking for the past, so I spent a lot of time in graveyards. I finally found a graveyard with a good number of Bradys but what jolted me was one particular grave stone. That family grave contained five people, buried over a span of some eighty years, each of whom was a Brady and each of whom was either born on or had died on my calendar date of birth – 10 March. As a member of my large, extended Irish-Australian family, I had always thought that I was the only Pisces, let alone the only person born on 10 March. I had considered that my birth date was unique to me, my particular contribution to the family zodiacal patterns. Instead I found myself looking at an unfolding pattern across time, generations and countries. My sun's zodiacal position was a small part of a fractal, iterating over time, always a little different but always similar and I was a small part of this fractal. As an adjunct to this story, I recently had a great nephew, also with the surname of Brady, born on the 10 March, so the pattern continues. ‑ 10 March, 10 March, 10 March.

Is this unique or rare? The short answer is no. Every family has its own repeating patterns. The third son killed in war for three generations, the members of a family all born or dying on the same day of the week, daughters mirroring mothers in giving birth to the same number of children, same gender of children, divorcing at the same age or in the number of marriages they make, and so on. Some of these patterns may be destructive and some may be constructive and some may simply be a curiosity, as in my own example.

Until Mandelbrot's work in fractals, these family patterns were disregarded as insignificant, idiosyncratic, non-explainable, shoulder-shrugging coincidences. However, now chaotic psychology acknowledges that families reproduce the same style of events over many generations. All families have patterns and just as a family has patterns, so too can an individual's life. Currently some psychological thought is that our lives unfold in a fractal like manner and far from being seen as odd, meaningless and at times superstitious, these family or personal reproductions of patterns or events are to be expected[9]. Fractals are not the games of mathematicians but are potentially the simple expression of the dynamics of life and time captured in an image.

Unpacking the language of Chaos

The twists and turns, the odd events, the coincidences, the serendipities of life that we all accept as the ebb and flow of our daily lives do have parallels with the twists and turns, repeating themes and emerging patterns of fractals and a system in chaos; and since astrology, like fractals, also deals with the patterns of life, then to explore any potential parallels between astrology and chaos we need to first encounter the language of chaos. Additioanlly, we can use the exploration of simpler chaotic systems as a window to look into the more complicated chaotic systems of our own lives.

Two types of Chaos – Entropic and Deterministic

According to the Fables of Aesop:

> …there once lived two frogs who were neighbours.
> The one inhabited a deep pond, far removed from
> public view; the other lived in a gully containing

---

[9] see R.Abraham. *Chaos, Gaia, Eros* :215. and see M.Butz. *Chaos and Complexity – Implications for Psychological Theory and Practice*: 4.

little water, and traversed by a country road. He that
lived in the pond warned his friend, and entreated
him to change his residence, and to come and live
with him, saying that he would enjoy greater safety
from danger and more abundant food. The other
refused, saying that he felt it so very hard to remove
from a place to which he had become accustomed.
A few days afterwards a heavy wagon passed through
the gully, and crushed him to death under its
wheels[10].

This fable shows us two pathways open to the frog in the gully:
one is to take a risk and travel to the new and hopefully better
pond; the other is the pathway of stagnation without change
which, the fables teaches us, leads to death. This is summarized
in the saying, "The groove becomes the rut becomes the grave"
as much as it is within chaos theory: the stable, unchanging
state defined as entropic chaos leads to no new patterns while
the state of change and thus encountering upheaval leads to
deterministic chaos full of new patterns and new opportunities.

By the late 20th century economists discovered that all
economies needed to be flexible, for if an economy stayed stable
and was not allowed to change, then that economy was pushed
towards entropic chaos - the frog in the gully - and this was
the road to stagnation and depression[11]. However, if economies
were intentionally pushed gently into unstable situations, then
new patterns emerged from the turbulence which led to greater
options or greater diversity, like the frog in the deep pond.
This idea of moving a system consciously into deterministic
chaos is now being applied across many diverse disciplines

---

[10] *The Fables of Aesop*, London: The Folio Society: 91.
[11] see M.Waldrop. *Complexity: The Emerging Science at the Edge of Order
and Chaos*.

from economics to people management to family therapy to the health and even the lifestyle of individuals[12].

This is not a new idea. From our own life experience we instinctively know that by allowing change, by ruffling our comfort zone, by taking a few risks, we open ourselves to new patterns and new opportunities. We already know and understand the difference between deterministic and entropic chaos. The actor Milton Berle (1908-2002) also knew this when he said: "If opportunity doesn't knock, build a door." This is a basic axiom of life, that it must have change and that opportunities can only be created by such change.

Complexity – a place where creation happens

When economists recognised that a stable economy tended towards stagnation which tended towards depression, they knew they needed a new approach. Yet most governments and companies find it unwise to push a stable, economic system tending towards stasis into complete chaos, as the drama involved in the emergence of new economic patterns would be considerable. Indeed when this occurs in political systems it is called a revolution and whilst eventually yielding new patterns and order, it does so via tremendous loss of life and human suffering. Thus in the 1990s some economists were focused on finding just how much an economy needed to be "disturbed" in order for it to start to yield new patterns.

The results from this research revealed that, as in the closed system of fractals, there is a thin zone between stasis and total breakdown. It is in this thin zone located on the edge of chaos, just before a system goes chaotic (totally unpredictable), that order naturally occurred and complexity

---

[12] J.van Eenwyk. *Archetypes and Strange Attractors*: 45; M.Butz. *Chaos and Complexity – Implications for Psychological Theory and Practice*: 18.

increased with no apparent cause[13]. The study of this thin zone where new patterns emerged in open systems (systems where all the variables were not known) was named Complexity. We can observe simple versions of this thin zone of complexity in the shapes of fractals, the images (*see figures 5, 6 and 7*) that are formed at the edges between light and dark. This thin line in the fractal erupts with patterns, shapes, images, and order.

As it is with fractals, so too we see this in living systems. Complexity research has found that in economies, communities, family groups or just one person's life new order emerges when the system is ruffled by increasing its networks, by moving it a little away from its established orderly systems, by pushing it gently towards "the edge of chaos". As we move the system towards turbulence or a time of potency where it can be tripped by what is known in complexity as a tipping point[14], so the system enters a fertile zone, a tiny phase of transition between a place of no change and a place of total change, and it is in this place that new patterns, new opportunities and new ideas emerge. The "edge of chaos" is not *an edge of chaos*, a place of upheaval but rather, in complexity, it is the phase or zone where even the smallest of changes at the right time can produce a cascade of new order. This new order is not the simple rearrangement of existing components into a new format but rather is a new scheme made up of previously unknown elements. These new patterns are self-emergent, neither created by a designer nor drafted out as rough

---

[13] Stuart Kauffman. (1991). "Antichaos and adaptation", in *Scientific American*, 256 (2), 78-84; S.Kauffman. *At Home in the Universe: The Search for the Laws of Self-Organization and Complexity*:15; E. Corcoran. "The Edge of Chaos"; M.Waldrop. *Complexity: The Emerging Science at the Edge of Order and Chaos*.
[14] *see* Malcolm Gadwell. (2000). *The Tipping Point: How Little Things Can Make a Big Difference*. Boston, MA: Little-Brown.

sketches and formed by an artisan hand, neither planned by management nor implemented by governments. This new order is out of nothing - *creatio ex nihilo*.

The emergence of the Internet is one example of *creatio ex nihilo*. Conceived as a potential for linking the world, it was "designed" by artisans and first connected in October 1969 with two computers between UCLA and Stanford Research Institute. It then grew and developed into an open network system, providing a super-rich feedback environment where "un-designed" and "un-planned" new order began to emerge. The concept of e-commerce, e-mail, virtual communities, on-line groups, local business being able to sell to the world and the resulting social implications are all forms of new order which did not exist prior to the development of the Internet. These are concepts that have emerged via the complexity of the network.

The study of relationship-rich open systems (the number of variables are unknown) is generally the area of complexity science and the study of relationship-rich semi-closed systems (where a number of variables are known), is generally the domain of chaos theory.

Bifurcations and Saddle Points - The time and place of change

Chaotic systems including life are full of changes, decisions and cross-roads. Whether these chaotic systems are a simple formula being iterated to create a fractal (closed system), a weather system full of variables engaged in producing a weather pattern or an individual person struggling to decide between employment opportunities (open system), they will all contain bifurcations and saddle points – times when decisions need to be made.

Hamlet, in his role of Everyman, voiced such a dilemma when he said:

> To be, or not to be: that is the question:
> Whether 'tis nobler in the mind to suffer
> The slings and arrows of outrageous fortune,
> Or to take arms against a sea of troubles,
> And by opposing end them?...[15]

In the language of chaos, the fork when the pattern or system can leap one way or the other is called a bifurcation. Hamlet is at a bifurcation point, pondering whether he should take the pathway of risk, the pathway to deterministic chaos, or whether to turn his steps to entropic chaos and let all things end. Of course Shakespeare propels Hamlet into deterministic chaos, for without that decision there is no story, no drama and no new patterns that can unfold and shape the destiny of his characters. Aesop's fable about the two frogs has one of the frogs reaching a time of bifurcation – to leave his pond or not to leave. He chooses no change, which leads to entropic chaos and thus he dies, causing the fable to end. No new story, no new patterns, no new adventures.

When a bifurcation can potentially change the whole pattern it is called a hopf bifurcation named after its discoverer, Polish mathematician Heinz Hopf (1894-1971). We could say that Hamlet is at a hopf bifurcation because his chosen pathway allows a whole new pattern to emerge. In 49 B.C.E. Julius Caesar crossed the river Rubicon and in doing so, broke the Roman law which forbade any general with a standing army to cross this river. The river marked the boundary between the province of Cisalpine, Gaul, to the north and the Roman heartland to the south and the law was to protect the republic from internal military threat. When Caesar crossed this river with his army, he knew there was no turning back. He was engaging on a pathway of conflict with the Republic and it would herald great change for him personally, either death or

---

[15] Hamlet 3:1, 58-62

glory. Julius Caesar was at a personal hopf bifurcation and his actions lead to determinstic chaos but this was also a hopf bifurcation for the history of Western civilization, for this action heralded the birth of the Roman Empire and one of the geneses of modern European culture.

The Rubicon was the place where the bifurcation occurred. Bifurcations will occur at a time or a place and, whether physical or mathematical, this place is called a saddle point: two pathways offered to the evolving pattern - person or equation - one of which will lead to an ending, the other to whole new patterns and order. For Napoleon, the battlefield of Waterloo was a saddle point and the choices he made placed him on a pathway of reduced options. For the American colonists in 1773, a ship in Boston harbour loaded with tea was another saddle point and the choices taken there led to the nation of the United States of America.

Areas of psychology are also adopting these new findings from chaos theory, seeing changes in people's lives expressed as encountering bifurcations and saddle points[16]. Within this thinking it is believed that if a person seeks too much stability or order in their life, they may, as they encounter their bifurcations, constantly bias themselves into entropic chaos. This person's life becomes one where no new opportunities present themselves and no new ideas are allowed to enter their world. They lead a life which slowly grinds down into a smaller and smaller milieu until death. In contrast to this, if a person seeks or accepts some of the risk presented by the bifurcations in their life and actively engages in periods of disorder so that new patterns can emerge, then the person's life will produce

---

[16] see M Butz. *Chaos and Complexity – Implications for Psychological Theory and Practice*; K.Mainzer. *Thinking in Complexity: The complex dynamics of matter, mind and mankind*; J.van Eenwyk. *Archetypes and Strange Attractors*.

new opportunities and be the richer for it, filled with new ventures, ideas and excitement.

But there is something else at work here, something working from within which encapsulates our goals, dreams and aspirations and which pulls us towards them and thus towards our own personal bifurcations. These are called attractors.

Attractors, Strange and otherwise

We are all attracted to things, people and ideas. Indeed this concept of attraction is the same idea of *logos* which was the principle that Heraclitus suggested in the 6th century B.C.E. It is our attractions which pull us forward through life. If we harbour avarice, then we are attracted to what we see but cannot acquire; if we are filled with love for another, then we are attracted towards a person and seek to know and understand them; if we are attracted to a place, we wish to spend time there; if we are attracted to an idea, we wish to focus on its potential. We live our life by our attractions which motivate us and pull us through our life.

Chaos theory also has attractors. Indeed chaos theory recognises three main types of attractors. The simplest is a point attractor - a funnel with all the fluids running to the centre. The next is a periodic attractor - bodies with a periodic oscillation. The planets orbiting around the sun have the sun as their periodic attractor. We can see these first two types of attractors in the everyday objects around us, water running down the drain, a point attractor, or the second hand on a watch face, doomed to sweep around and around the watch face, forever tied by an arm to its periodic attractor, the centre pin. But there is third type of attractor which describes another type of action.

If we are at a circus watching acrobats flipping and flying through the air on horizontal bars hanging by ropes, we totally understand the scene we are watching. Now pretend the trapeze is invisible. What we would now see could seem quite strange indeed: people moving through the air, swinging around one point, flying off to another point and all of these points bending and curving with nothing staying still. Simplistic as is this example, we would be watching the effect of what chaoticians calls a strange attractor. The effect is the movement of the acrobats; the strange attractor is the invisible structure of the trapeze.

When a person embedded in classical science observes a chaotic system, the unfolding pattern of events will appear to be quite random. However, if the system's movement can be plotted graphically, far from being random, such movements will be seen to orbit around a set of multidimensional foci. Such foci are like the bars and rings used by the acrobats in the flying trapeze circus act. If we plotted the movement of the trapeze artist, we would discover the two swinging foci of the invisible trapeze bars. In chaos theory these moving foci points are known as strange attractors. Strange attractors exist in chaotic systems and can be found by observing the patterns produced within a system. Such a system can be in mathematics (closed system) or it can be a single life, a collection of ants, a company, or an economy (open system). All of these will produce and contain strange attractors[17].

Lorenz' famous butterfly and weather example came about when he plotted the apparent random results of his equations and produced an image in the shape of a butterfly. Each "eye" on a wing was a focal point of the strange attractor (*see figure 8*). However, these strange attractors are a great deal more than just interesting patterns, for chaos research implies that the relationship of life with other lives and life with its environment results in the creation of strange

---

[17] F. Capra. *The Web of Life: A New Scientific Understanding of Living Systems*: 132.

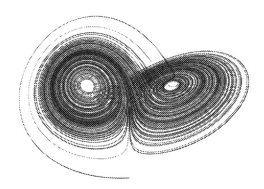

Figure 8 – The Lorenz butterfly strange attractor. The "trapeze" around which Lorenz' computer-modelled weather experiment was orbiting.

attractors. Once formed these strange attractors act as foci directing the unfolding events and over time produce patterns that are scale-invariant and self-similar[18]. Indeed according to the findings of chaos theory and complexity, life and all that supports life functions by being influenced by, and orbiting around, strange attractors[19]. This claim has large implications, for it suggests that there is no such thing as random behaviour, neither for a person's life, a community, an economy, or history nor any other rich feedback system. We all orbit around strange attractors. Strange attractors are the "ghosts in the machine".[20] We cannot see them but they are in fact what shape the events in any chaotic system.

Sections of psychology have embraced the concepts of strange attractors and see them as the invisible hand in an unfolding life, directing it in what appears for an observer to

---

[18] J.van Eenwyk. *Archetypes and Strange Attractors*: 48.
[19] K.Mainzer. *Thinking in Complexity: The complex dynamics of matter, mind and mankind*: 264-265; I.Prigogine and I.Stengers. *Order Out of Chaos: Man's New Dialogue with Nature*.:121; M.Butz. *Chaos and Complexity – Implications for Psychological Theory and Practice*:21.
[20] With apologise to Gilbert Ryle (1900-1976) who first used this term in his attack on the dualism of Rene Descarte.

be random but what is actually a precise set of patterns. In family therapy, strange attractors are considered to be visible in what could be called family curses or family gifts. A family that was continually beset with illness or general misfortune over several generations would, in this model, be said to have within their midst a difficult strange attractor. In contrast, the 17th century German musical family, the Bachs, showed a powerful musical strange attractor where, in a two hundred year period, four branches of the family tree came under its influence.

We gain strange attractors in many ways. It may be that we are born into them through family, culture or nationality, or we may create our own through living our life and forming associations with others. We know, for example, that our friendships are important and that an association with some people may open us to strange attractors which pull us into areas and ideas we enjoy. On the other hand, by associating with "bad" company we may collide with unpleasant and unwelcome situations. When you accept a new strange attractor into your life, consciously or unconsciously, you open yourself and your life to new patterns. You encounter this new order or new patterns through the drama of encountering the "edge of chaos", which complexity research suggests could be seen as simply a tiny event that leads smoothly to new patterns. Nevertheless, however you encounter this new order, you begin to take different actions, drive down different streets, go to different places, think different thoughts, eat different foods and meet different people.

Jungian psychologist van Eenwyk links strange attractors with the concept of archetypes in an individual's or community's life. He suggests that myths are verbal fractals showing different choices (bifurcations), some leading to loss and destruction (entropic chaos) and others leading to fruitfulness (deterministic chaos). The end result of such a story is often a new strange attractor found or created and taken back to the tribe[21].

We know little about strange attractors except that they exist in chaotic systems (all of life), that we experience them in our own life as a motivation or a pulling towards an idea or event, and that over time they produce patterns in our behaviour.

We also know that all attractors have a zone of influence and this zone of influence is called a basin.

Basins – your little black book

In a single point attractor the zone of influence or basin is the size of the funnel. Any fluid or object that finds itself in the funnel is drawn toward the single point attractor. The basin of the periodic attractor of our solar system is defined as the gravity of the sun which creates an area that draws other bodies into orbital pathways around it. We know, for example, that Pluto was captured by wandering into our sun's basin.

The basin of a strange attractor is thus the orb of influence of the attractor and some chaoticians believe that bifurcations occur in the zone where the basin of one strange attractor overlaps another. When Julius Caesar crossed the Rubicon, he had reached a saddle point which gave him two pathways (bifurcations). He could choose to stay motivated by his current goals (in chaotic language he could continue to stay in the basin of his current strange attractor) or he could leave this familiar basin and move into deterministic chaos, (the boundary between one strange attractor and another) and enter the "gravitational pull" of a new strange attractor. This new strange attractor encompassed both the actual city of Rome as well as the desire to control the Roman Republic and become ruler of the known world. The day when Julius Caesar

---

[21] J.van Eenwyk. *Archetypes and Strange Attractors*: 120.

first thought of marching on Rome was the day when he first felt "the pull" of the new strange attractor.

We all have different types of attractors in our life and they all have basins. Their size, their times of change and our acknowledgement of their presence are all important occupations for living a healthy life. We play team sports by firstly designing a semi-closed system (the game's rules) which dictates the type of events that can emerge and then intentionally overlap the basins of two point attractors (opposing side's soccer nets, or basketball hoops, and so on). We add to the potential tension between the two attractors two teams (the open relationship-rich network part of the system that can create new order) who are set against each other by supporting opposite attractors. With this half open system (the teams) and half closed system (the rules) we then sit back and enjoy watching the unscripted drama (new order) which spontaneously emerges.

When we endanger a species by damaging its habitat, we are effectively reducing its basin and therefore its options and moving it closer to entropic chaos (extinction). Similarly if we place an individual into solitary confinement, we are dramatically reducing their basin and forcible damaging their pattern-making-life-systems, visiting punishment upon them by pushing them closer to entropic chaos. We have conflict when we unintentionally overlap basins with others. We naturally seek to expand our basin but also seek the right balance between stagnation (too small a basin) and stress (too large or too many basins). We place attractors in our life, like a new interest or a new friendship, but in doing so we must find a place in our collection of basins where it can have "its own space" without draining other basins within our province.

Phase portraits – the overview of a chaotic system

There is one more important concept. Chaos theory has maps and these maps are called phase portraits. Generally a phase portrait will be used in a closed system and thus complexity science (complex open systems) considers them too limiting. However, astrology is a hybrid of both the mechanical world (based in the Newtonian solar system and thus a type of closed system) and the non-linear dynamic, complex world (an open system). The concepts of phase portraits may therefore have a special place in this unique hybrid model. Physicist and systems theorist Fritjof Capra defines phase portraits as a map of the unfolding potential of a particular pattern which can be used to gain understanding of the quality of a non-linear dynamic system. He says and it is worth noting his exact words:

> The qualitative analysis of a dynamic system, then, consists of identifying the system's attractors and basins of attraction, and classifying them in terms of their topological characteristics [ability to change], the result is a dynamical picture of the entire system, called the "phase portrait"[22].

Capra is saying that an unfolding pattern (which we could suggest is a person's life) can be mapped in terms of its attractors (psychology would call this the personality make up, family issues or parts of the self that pull events and people into the life). These attractors have basins, an individual's areas of influence such as their everyday life, their family or their entire email address book. These incorporate the nature and size of the physical, mental, emotional and spiritual areas of a person's life. The topological characteristics are a measure of how flexible and adaptable the person might be to the influence of the attractors. Such a map, Capra tells us, is called a phase

---

[22] F. Capra. *The Web of Life: A New Scientific Understanding of Living Systems*: 134.

portrait and it can be used for the qualitative analysis of the "system". He is working with a closed system but such a map has implications for open systems.

Astrology also has maps. Our maps are closed systems (the predictable movement of the planets) but we use them to draw parallels to human life (open systems) and we call them horoscopes. We read these maps to give us insights into the qualitative analysis of the person.

This language of chaos with its basins, attractors and bifurcations is providing new terms and understanding of the experience of life which has previously been devalued or dismissed. Until the advent of chaos theory, this intuitive knowledge has been without language and thus when voiced has had no authority. This is a key point. Chaos has not discovered new concepts but rather, through mathematics, is providing a language for the experience of life. Chaos is giving a language to the place outside the walled garden.

Chaos and Creation - The Philosophy of Antiquity	Chaos Theory	The qualitative experience of life
All things are linked and influence each other.	A system linked by positive feedback produces chaos. This is a non-linear dynamic system.	All life is in a continuous process of influencing its surroundings, while its surroundings influence it.
A large event can be linked to a small event and vice versa (omens and superstition).	Patterns are scale invariant.	The experience of linking two seemingly disconnected events can be labelled "coincidence" but for many people these occur too frequently in their life to be dismissed as containing no meaning.
Stories (myths) repeat themselves, events unfold as they have before.	Patterns unfold in a self-similar manner.	Myths, stories and archetypes will repeat in a person's life or the life of a family, company or country. This is termed "serendipity".
A pattern can be encouraged through ritual or other such practices. Actions at the beginning of an event can influence the outcome.	Sensitive dependence on initial conditions (SDIC). The "butterfly" effect. Tiny changes at the beginning of a pattern lead to disproportional differences later.	Small attitude changes in an individual or a small, seemingly insignificant change to one's daily routine can have huge consequences on the way one's life unfolds. This is usually understood in retrospect: "If I had not taken that different route to work that morning…" and so on.
There is a pattern which shapes all life – destiny or fate.	The nature of the unfolding pattern is influenced by the strange attractors within the system which "pull" it towards certain behaviours.	The experience of a guiding hand – the divine. The long string of coincidences which unfold in the correct manner. Teleology yielding an experience of the divine.

Figure 9 - a summary of chaos myths, chaos theory and the qualitative experience of life.

4

WHERE CHAOS MEETS ASTROLOGY

The practice of chaos theory and astrology both map the quality of a moment, chaos theory via phase portraits and astrology via horoscopes. Both consider the potential of a point in time, how an object or event at that moment in time will react to change, when it will be faced with changes and what will be its tendencies and behaviour when faced with these potential changes. For a phase portrait, the object can be a person's life or even a family dynamic[1] and so too for a horoscope. Whatever the object, the purpose of the map is to chart the future history of that object.

Let us take an example of an object and think about its phase portrait. Leonardo da Vinci (1452-1519) painted the *Mona Lisa* in oil on wood between 1503 and 1506. He carried it with him for years and finally took it to France, selling it in 1516 to King Francois I for 4,000 gold coins. Originally much larger than it is now, at some point after Leonardo's death the painting was cut down to its measurements of today of 31 x 21 inches (77 x 53 cm). The painting first resided in the Royal Château de Fontainebleau and then hung in the Palace of Versailles. For a while after the French revolution it graced the bedroom of Napoleon I in the Tuileries Palace and was then moved to the Louvre. It was hidden for safety during the Franco-Prussian War of 1870–1871 but between 1911 and 1913 it was stolen and hidden in a Louvre caretaker's apartment,

---

[1] see F.D. Abraham, R.H.Abraham and C.D. Shaw. (1990). A *visual introduction to dynamical systems theory for psychology*. Santa Cruz, CA: Aerial.

finally to be returned. During World War II it was removed once again from the Louvre for safe keeping. 1956 was the painting's most difficult year: someone attacked it with acid and someone also threw stones at it. In 1962-63 the painting was allowed to be exhibited in New York City and Washington D.C. and in 1974 it was exhibited in Tokyo and Moscow. Thereafter its passport was cancelled. It was returned to the Louvre for good to live out its days behind bullet proof glass.

If we were to draft out the phase portrait of the *Mona Lisa*, firstly it would contain materials - paint and wood. Once the physical piece was completed, we would place into its phase portrait the attractors and the size of their basins and any resulting saddle points with their bifurcations and topological characteristics (the painting's ability to adapt). All of this would then give us an insight into the unfolding potential story of the life of the *Mona Lisa*.

Leonardo's love of the painting was one major attractor and this expressed itself through him carrying the painting around with him for so many years. But there was another attractor – Leonardo's need for money which led him to sell it for 4,000 gold coins. When Leonardo's need for money increased and overlapped King Francois' attractor of his desire for the painting, they formed the saddle point, the potential place or point where change could occur and a whole new phase of the painting's history began. There are many other attractors to be plotted on the phase portrait of the *Mona Lisa*: the greed of the thieves in 1911, the fear for its protection during the wars, the anger of the attackers with acid and stone, and the desire of the world to see the painting causing it to travel to Japan, USA and Russia.

The *Mona Lisa*, with its mysterious beauty, is also an attractor in its own right and its reputation has created a huge basin. However, fear for its safety has caused it to be removed from encountering any further attractors, coming to saddle points or moving through bifurcations. Placed behind bullet proof glass, the physical painting has been moved into a state of entropic chaos. Yet the picture does spawn millions of copies of itself and this could be seen as a new phase of its life. Like fractals, these copies are self-similar but not exactly the same, all a little different not only in image but in media; mouse mats, coffee mugs, calendars, prints, clothing, postcards, key rings, and so on. There is also scale invariance but this time the scale is not just size but value and number: one *Mona Lisa* painting of immeasurable value, millions of *Mona Lisa* images of little value.

In our model the phase portrait for the *Mona Lisa* may only contain three initial attractors: Leonardo's love of the work, his highly valued skills as an artist, and his need for money. Yet by knowing these attractors, the phase portrait could note the saddle points and the potential pathways that might be taken by the bifurcations. Adding Leonardo's history of flexibility (his topological features) to all of this would then lead to us to be able to judge the nature of the unfolding story of the world's most famous painting. Collating the details of this phase portrait allows us to predict that Leonardo's need for money linked with his love of the painting and his exalted reputation will eventually lead him to sell the painting for a substantial sum of money. This sum may be so large that the painting would have to be sold to royalty and therefore find itself hanging in a palace. Ownership of the costly painting would thus bring prestige to the owner and this could eventually lead to the painting becoming a national treasure. However, at any of these bifurcations the painting could chose entropic chaos and become destroyed by fire, acid or revolution and join the catalogue of lost treasures. What is important here is that given the simplicity of the initial phase portrait, we can predict the quality of the future of the painting but not its exact story.

An astrologer on the other hand would look to the horoscope for the *Mona Lisa* for this information. This would be the chart for that moment when Leonardo started work on his first few sketches in a notebook on a summer's day in Florence. If the chart was known, and provided the painting did not at any stage move into entropic chaos, the astrologer would expect to be able to see represented in this chart the great size of the basin that the *Mona Lisa* would eventually create, the times of selling, hiding, attacks and injuries, times of travel, and its extraordinary ability to reproduce itself. For astrologers consider that the initial conditions of the sky and the earth set for the beginning of the emergence of new order is the moment that contains its story.

So is a horoscope a form of phase portrait? It would seem that astrologers use them in the same manner to which Capra refers for their use and expectation. But is this just an illusion?

The Horoscope and the Phase Portrait

A phase portrait is a detailed understanding of the initial conditions and embraces what is defined in chaos theory as SDIC – Sensitive Dependant to Initial Conditions. This is the principle where extremely small changes to the initial conditions lead to disproportional differences as events move away from their initial moment of commencement. Tiny changes in Lorenz' weather variables lead to totally different and unpredictable weather patterns. Within the discipline of psychology it has actually been suggested that an astrological chart *could* be considered a form of SDIC[2] as it maps some of the details of the initial conditions at the moment of the emergence of

---

[2] J.van Eenwyk. *Archetypes and Strange Attractors*: 115.

the new order. Additionally, since astrologers also consider that any small changes to the map – the time or the place – can lead to huge changes in the unfolding story defined by the map, it would appear that whilst the components of the map are different, the activity and intent of the astrologer and the chaotician are the same.

Is this sufficient evidence to see horoscopes as early proto-phase portraits? There is yet another major correlation. As explored in the previous chapter, the work in complexity is concerned with exploring the thin phase that is formed when relationships are increased in a network and begin to move between a solid unchanging state and a place of total dispersal. Complexity research found that in the space of this tiny membrane, entropy appears to reverse and new order spontaneously emerges. These findings have filtered into molecular biology which also indicates that life began in this manner: a relationship-rich soup in which new order, some of which reproduces itself over time and over different scales, began to emerge[3]. Now there are strong parallels between the thin phases studied by complexity and the thin membrane of the biosphere where all life emerged. Both are a thin phase bounded by either earth-space (biosphere) or unchanging – infinity (fractal). The biosphere produces diversity of life and the fractal produces diversity of pattern. Indeed one can argue that the biosphere is actually a phase space where complexity (increases in diversity) occurs and thus it can also be argued that the biosphere is a fractal-like space (*see figure 10*). Therefore we should not be surprised to discover that life itself behaves like a fractal unfolding in order and repeating patterns[4].

---

[3] S.Kauffman. *At Home in the Universe: The Search for the Laws of Self-Organization and Complexity*: 15; F.Capra. *The Web of Life: A New Scientific Understanding of Living Systems*:209 – 211.

[4] ibid:209 – 211.

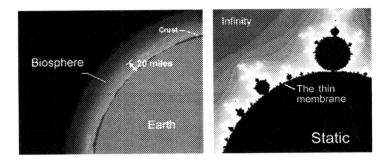

Figure 10 : Left - The biosphere is only twenty miles wide and exists between the earth and the infinity of space. It is the place where all known life (patterns and order) exists. Right - A fractal formed by spontaneous order and patterns in the thin membrane that exists between the static, unchanging conditions and the zone of infinity. Just as a fractal unfolds in the space of a thin membrane in self-similarity and scale invariance so, too, life on earth is considered to unfold in the biosphere via the same principles of self-similarity and scale invariance.

Astrologers map a thin slice of time and into this map of time they place the earth and the sky and then focus that map on the individual born at that moment. Astrologers therefore map a thin slice of the meeting of earth, sky and time. Astrology has been drawing these qualitative maps of a person's initial starting conditions for several thousand years and these maps are of the relationship between three areas: *static* (earth)/ *complexity zone* (biosphere)/*zone of total dispersal* (sky). Furthermore these maps are preoccupied with the SDIC of the new emergent order, as they are set for the exact time and place of birth. Astrology is, in effect, mapping the very place where chaos theory indicates that new order emerges in a self-similar and scale invariant manner.

Chaotic psychology acknowledges the fractal like nature of our lives but draws away from, or fails to address, the idea supported by chaos theory of the importance of SDIC in relationship to life. Yet through the discoveries of chaos theory, we know that the initial conditions at the time of the emergence of new order is of key importance to how that new order will unfold. So if the findings of chaos theory have significance for the way human life unfolds, we can argue that the unfolding pattern of a human's life *is* indeed sensitive to its initial conditions. Thus by analogy, astrology's preoccupation with the initial conditions at the moment of birth of an individual is arguably a justifiable position, since one cannot have some of the principles of chaos without all of them.

Thus it is possible that the tools of astrology which intuitively and empirically developed some three thousand years ago do actually have some merit. It is possible to consider the horoscope as a justifiable, albeit simple, map of the initial conditions of the emerging new life on "the edge of chaos" which seeks to show its quality and future potential.

From a chaotic perspective, a criticism one could make of these ideas is that the horoscope may be too simple, containing too thin a slice of information. A chaotician may want many other variables when constructing a phase portrait for that moment of emergence; yet in principle there seems to be little difference between the two. However, regardless of whether one accepts this argument that horoscopes have a strong correlation with chaos' idea of a phase portrait, there are other correlations which can be explored between astrology and chaos.

Planetary Patterns and Strange Attractors

Every horoscope contains what astrologers call planetary patterns. These are the geometrical patterns formed between the planets and the surface of the earth at the time of the person's birth as viewed from the earth. Depending on the type of astrology being practised, these are thought to be particular markers or tendencies within the person's life or within the person's psyche which will dictate, symbolize or indicate their behaviour patterns. Chaos studies within psychology acknowledge the existence of such behavioural tendencies and label them as strange attractors[5].

Putting this into astrological language, if a person is born with a Moon – Pluto pattern, then astrologers believe that the person will draw unto themselves the nature of this planetary pair. Issues of trust, betrayal and intense relationships will be a feature of their life. There will be many different expressions of this tendency but a planetary pattern, to an astrologer is what a chaotic psychologist would define as a strange attractor. It shapes the unfolding pattern of the person's life, guiding who they meet, the situations in which they find themselves and the way they react to events. However, an important difference is that via the tool of the horoscope, the astrologer can actually see and recognise the "astrological" strange attractor. The psychologist, on the other hand, can only become aware of the "psychological" strange attractor by observing its influence over a long period of time.

This point becomes more obvious if we run it backwards. Astrologers may encounter a person's biography and conclude through the life story that a particular planetary combination is at work in the person's horoscope. Consider the following client's story emailed to me in 2005[6]. Anne (not her real name) is talking about her partner:

> I've lived in hope for way too long but his total
> personality change from loving, happy and positive
> to nit picking, dragging up the past over and over
> and just being a nasty person when he doesn't have
> his treatment for weeks on end, is affecting my
> health and business. I have been told that he'll
> eventually self destruct as he seems hell bent on

---

[5] see J.van Eenwyk. *Archetypes and Strange Attractors*.
[6] Personal email and quoted with permission.

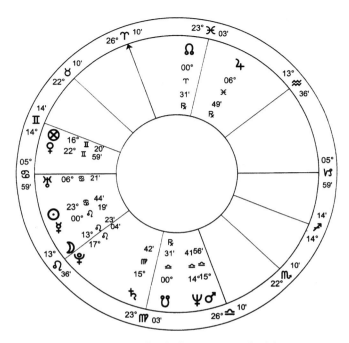

Figure 11 – "Anne" – birth data not supplied for privacy

totally neglecting himself. …. And everyone says
only death will separate us! .. but I have a feeling it
is all coming apart as I can't take any more abuse
one day then love and affection the next.

What is the planetary pattern at work here? What are the
strange attractors? It is not relevant that Anne is talking about
her partner. Anne herself is in this situation and has been for
ten years. She is therefore living within the basin of a particular
strange attractor which provides her with an intense, dramatic,
till-death-do-us-part relationship which swings wildly from
loving and tender to resentment, anger and abuse. An
astrologer would not be surprised to learn that she is born
with Uranus on her Ascendant and a Moon-Pluto conjunction,
(*see her chart in figure 11*). These are two strange attractors

with over-lapping basins, one for independence and the other for intense bonding and Anne's life, via her relationship, moves in and out of their basins of influence.

Whilst there is a great deal more which can be considered in her chart, for Anne this particular pattern results in a see-saw of turmoil in her partner's behaviour. Anne does not cause this see-saw, instead she draws into her life someone who can provide this for her and she oscillates between the two attractors in a stuck state. In chaotic terms, she is in a form of entropic chaos. Such a state can be helped by Anne increasing her networks which would allow new patterns to emerge and provide opportunities for her to see fresh solutions to her problems. This approach to Anne's dilemma is the practice of chaotic astrology, dealt with in more detail later. At this stage, however, it is simply important to understand and see the workings of these psychological and/or astrological strange attractors in Anne's life.

Here is another example. In 2005, 'Joan' wrote me the following email:

> I am working with a recurring pattern/cycle in my life which has hit me once more. In this cycle I feel totally lost, like I am in a whirlpool being sucked down, with no idea what I want, what to do, just wanting to withdraw from people, and everyday tasks like cooking or shopping feel overwhelming, and I'm left wondering what the point of life is, but at the same time I feel a real urgency to do something or latch on to something to pull me out of it.
> … it doesn't feel like me[7].

No astrologer would be surprised to learn that Joan has a Sun-Neptune conjunction on her 12th house cusp (*See her chart in figure 12*).

---

[7] Personal email and quoted with permission.

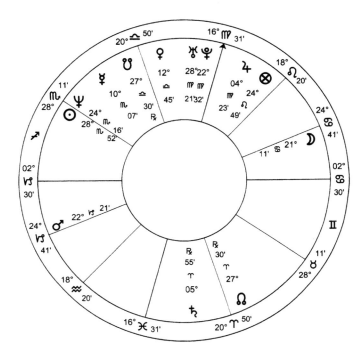

Figure 12 - "Joan" - birth data not supplied for privacy

Joan acknowledges that this is one of her cycles but as she becomes drawn into the basin of the Sun-Neptune strange attractor, she finds that she has no skills to understand it and simply experiences the movement into its basin as being "sucked down" into a whirlpool. Both Anne and Joan, by their own words, are talking about a persistent difficulty which seems beyond their control.

If we define a strange attractor in the manner of a chaotic psychologist as a hidden influence which dictates or influences behaviour, then both Anne and Joan are talking about strange attractors which have immense ramifications on their lives. Like a psychologist seeing a neurosis, an astrologer can recognise and label these patterns. However, to the astrologer's eye the strange attractor is not hidden but can be seen in the map for the moment of birth.

Astrologers acknowledge and incorporate into their practice the concepts of strange attractors (as defined within chaotic psychology) by accepting that certain horoscopic features will pull the individual into different repeating patterns.

Saddle Points and the Sensitive Points of a Horoscope

A saddle point is a place where a system is sensitive to change, a point where at some future time a fork in the path appears and the unfolding life or equation has to "decide" between options. It is important to appreciate that the options open to the unfolding life or equation are *not* infinite. Indeed according to the findings of chaos theory, there are only a limited number of options available at the saddle point and resulting bifurcation. In astrological language, we can see a saddle point as a sensitive point in the natal horoscope and when these points become emphasised by some predictive technique, such as a transit, then this is the time in which changes will occur in the person's life. The nature of the changes which will occur for the person will, as both chaos theory and astrology suggests, be finite, not infinite.

Using chaotic terms, Anne's email (page 90) tells us that she thinks she has reached a saddle point. A bifurcation is opening up and she feels that she must "jump" but is unsure of what lies ahead of her. She wants change as she recognises the destructive nature of the entropic chaos she is in but she wants to encourage the change in as positive a manner as possible. There were quite a few transits to Anne's chart in 2005 but one transit in particular was transiting Pluto opposing her natal Venus. Most astrologers would note this as the active component in the system. Her natal Venus is the saddle point, being a sensitive horoscope point, and Anne's arrival at this bifurcation is indicated by Pluto forming a transiting opposition to it.

An astrologer can look at Anne's proto-phase portrait (horoscope) and see that in the year 2005 she will find herself drawn towards a bifurcation (a time of change). This time of change is not infinite in its possible outcomes, for the planetary combinations (strange attractors) indicate that at this time hidden or old issues (12th house Venus) connected with her intense personal relationship (Moon-Pluto conjunction) will reach a crisis. How a person can help this move towards deterministic chaos (a pattern rich, creative place) rather than entropic chaos is a subject to be dealt with later.

Astrologers acknowledge and incorporate into their practice the concepts of saddle points by recognising sensitive points in the horoscope which are used to predict future changes in both timing as well as quality.

Homeostasis – our resistance to change

In biology and in chaos theory one of the features of life is its ability to display resistance to small changes[8]. This is known as homeostasis, the ability of a richly-coupled, inter-relating network (life) to maintain itself in a world of continual adjustments. You have a certain balance in your life and you will naturally resist changes to that balance. Genererally, small events are not going to upset you or the flow of your life; however, large events can suddenly swing your life in new directions. You have homeostasis emotionally, spiritually, physically and intellectually. You may call them your boundaries; chaos calls them your homeostatic tendencies.

---

[8] S. Kauffman. *At Home in the Universe: The Search for the Laws of Self-Organization and Complexity* :79.

Astrologers also acknowledge a person's ability to resist change, as not all predictive events are seen as equal in their potential for heralding change. If Anne, for example, was experiencing transiting Venus opposing her natal Pluto, would she find herself at a bifurcation point? No, simply because the Venus transit to her natal Pluto is a frequent transit and, like a gentle breeze which blows often, it has little impact on Anne's ability to maintain her homeostasis. However, the Pluto transit is far less frequent, indeed it only occurs once in her entire life and as such it is like a force ten gale that howls into her world, showing the astrologer that this is when irreversible change will occur. Thus Anne's homeostasis is going to be seriously challenged. Indeed just as chaoticians are creating a bifurcation encyclopaedia[9], astrologers also have a corpus focused on this very subject. Any recognised published works on predictive astrology[10] will reflect this idea of firstly, grading different chart points for their sensitivity to change and secondly, grading predictive catalysts for their ability to indicate the magnitude of that change.

Astrologers acknowledge and incorporate the concept of homeostasis into their practice by grading the effect on a person's life of different predictive events.

Astrology's use of cycles - self-similarity and scale invariance

We live our life in a sea of time and, for many of us, it would seem that time comes but once. We are told that we must not waste it and we never seem to have enough of it and in our busy, self-absorbed world, we are lead to believe that time is linear and once gone, is lost forever. This may be true biologically in terms of your age and body but it is not true in

---

[9] R.Abraham. *Chaos, Gaia, Eros*:61.
[10] See B.Brady. *The Eagle and the Lark*; N.A.Hastings. *Secondary Progressions*; R.Ebertin. *Directions, Co-Determinants of Fate*.

terms of how we experience the world. Time is linear for material objects but for living systems it is experienced as cyclic and just as there are two worlds – linear and non-linear – there are in fact two types of time.

All our time-indicators are cyclic; some belong to large cycles, while others belong to much shorter cycles. The two fundamental indicators are firstly, the orbit of the earth around the sun which gives us the period of a year; and secondly, the rotation of the earth on its own axis which gives us the day. These are the bases of all *time*, no matter how we measure it, yet both of these measuring sticks have variations in them that remind our time-conscious world that time is not as constant and linear as we pretend. Even our atomic clocks have to pay homage to the irregular orbit of the earth, for every few years the manual adjustment of a leap second is required.

So time is not based on a linear concept and thus in its quality it does not visit us but once like a finite piece of string stretching off into the distance. Rather it is created in a circular fashion like a loop with a memory which constantly visits us again and again. You *do* get a second chance with the quality of time and events, sometimes even a third and fourth chance. Time, for living entities, is really cycles within cycles.

If we consider each annual cycle to be similar, then spring is spring, your birthday occurs at a certain time of the year and national holidays occur in an annual pattern. Some of these cycles are obvious. Every Monday you may do a particular task, so it is easy for you to predict approximately what you will be doing next Monday. Every summer you can predict warmer weather because the year unfolds in a precise way that you can experience and understand. You can remember past summers and can therefore anticipate future summers. Christmas Day may fall on a Wednesday but for many people they already know that it will not be a normal working

Wednesday due to *that* Wednesday's location in the larger cycle of the year. Yet through our history and the events of our lives, we recognise that each year, although similar, will also be different and unpredictable.

Despite all of this we tend to think of a year as a complete cycle, seeing it as independent and disconnected to other years, as the linear dynamic world in which we live only acknowledges the cycle of day and night, the cycle of a week and the cycle of the seasons. So our "cycle memory" can extend from an hour to a week day to a year but struggles to go beyond that. But to an astrologer time is different. The astrologer sees a person's life unfolding in repeating cycles, all a little different but all having a similar ambience and many of them being much longer than one year.

A cycle can be defined as the marriage of events with time, like a woven cloth where each thread and colour contributes to the design. The fabric itself is static but as it is woven, the order and sequence of the weave is just as much a part of the pattern as the actual colours of the threads. As we move our eye through the patterns of the cloth, we anticipate the next swirl by understanding the previous patterns made by the marriage of thread and timing. A cycle, therefore, informs us not only of the possible content, the pattern, but also the possible timing of these future events. Astrologers use many cycles, all of which are based on one scale, normally planetary, linked with another scale, that of the life of the person (a country, an organisation, and so on). Furthermore, along with other disciplines, astrology sees all cycles as expressing the same rhythm: a beginning, a period of growth, a time of fullness and then a period of waning leading to a winter or an end point which in turn leads to a rebirth. Whether the cycle is the diurnal rhythm of a day and night over twenty four hours, the monthly rhythm of the lunar phases, the cycles of outer planets - returns or aspect - or the synodic cycles of two planets which may take hundreds of years, all cycles in astrology unfold with the same key stages, all expressing the same key concepts[11]. Thus the dawn of a new day which happens every 24 hours and lasts only a few minutes is linked with emerging. So, too, is the crescent phase of the moon which occurs every 29½ days and lasts but a few days. So, too, is the separating angle of 45^0 between Neptune and Pluto which occurs every 492 years and may last for 60 years. All cycles, brief or long, have the same stages and in this respect they are an example of scale invariance and self-similarity, all different but all similar, some small and some large.

Additionally, an event or pattern which occurs at one point of the cycle will be expected, by the principles of self-similarity, to re-emerge in essence at the same point in the cycle again. This is obvious in the rhythm of the week days - Monday mornings produce their same repeatable behaviour in an individual - but all cycles, not just the rhythm of a week or a season, are linked by their self-similar stages. So combining this with scale invariance, the astrologer is able to examine one great cycle in order to investigate another unfolding cycle. Indeed, some of the most interesting predictive work produced by astrologers has been by combining cycles in this way.

Some years ago I was asked to write an article[12] on the future of Australia for the coming year and, like most astrologers faced with that task, I turned to cycles. The year in question was 2001 and I noted that there was going to be a repeat of a particular lunar cycle (19 years and 9 to 11 days). The event which occurred in Australia some 19 years earlier

[11] Dane Rudhyar. (1967). *The Lunation Cycle*. Santa Fe, New Mexico: Aurora Press :3.
[12] Bernadette Brady. (2001). "2001 Cycles of Growth and Expansion." In *Astrolog*, editor Barbara McGregor. Sydney, Australia: Wellbeing. 5-10.

was the social upheaval of the Chamberlain case where a dingo had allegedly taken and eaten a baby. It was a most difficult time in Australia with the whole nation swept up in the drama of the debate about the baby's death – was it matricide or death by dingo? In the article I simply suggested that we would be revisiting this drama again in some manner in 2001. As it so happened, in the year 2001 a small boy was killed by a dingo on Fraser Island, Queensland. This was the only time since the Chamberlain case that a child had been killed by a dingo. However, thankfully, in this self-similar pattern none of the dingoes in the area were killed, nor was the mother accused of murdering her child.

There was also another interesting cycle. Saturn takes 29½ years to travel through the zodiac, so the year of 2001 was linked to 1971 as both had Saturn in the same place in the zodiac. 1971 was a difficult year for airlines in Australia and Qantas, the main international airline of Australia, was grounded because of threats by extortionists. Thus in the article I suggested that there would be another airline grounded by strikes or other causes. As it came to pass, in 2001 another major Australian airline (Ansett) was grounded and nearly lost its licence due to failure to maintain correct safety standards. This was the only time since 1971 that a national airline had been grounded in Australia.

There was one other year which caught my eye. In 1989 a major bank collapsed in Australia. Jupiter has a 12 year cycle, so to my astrologer's eye the year 1989 was linked to 2001 with the quality of financial loss or company collapse. In 2001 a major insurance company (HIH Insurance) collapsed with a loss of five billon dollars.

These are all examples of scale invariance and self-similarity. One can cite hundreds of similar examples by astrologers across the world, as these are standard tools in any predictive astrologer's tool box. The astrologer first uses scale invariance to examine the nature of a forthcoming period of time by looking at another pattern, generally that of planetary configurations, then looks at history and gains insights into the nature of previous events linked with this saddle point (point in a chart or point in the zodiac). Finally the astrologer looks at the next time that particular saddle point will be "activated" by the same planetary cycle and, using the principles of self-similarity and scale invariance, they predict both the time frame of a future event and the quality of the future event but not its exact expression.

Astrologers acknowledge and actively use the concepts of self-similarity and scale invariance in their work, not only with cycles but also in their fundamental assumption that the patterns and cycles of the heavens are reflective of the patterns and cycles of life on earth.

The immortality of the horoscope and patterns

We know that the patterns of fractals can move through time indefinitely over millions of iterations. When associated with the patterns of life, fractals can be seen to reflect the immortality of life, the unceasing cycle of birth, life and death that maintains a species. Astrologers also acknowledge the immortal nature of these patterns, for within astrology there is the belief that a horoscope never dies. This is reflected by the fairly universal astrological practice of working with historical horoscopes such as a country, a past battle or even a long since deceased individual and comparing these horoscopes with that of a current living individual in order to judge the nature of the relationship between the two. Astrologers do not consider that biological death or the passing of time ends a pattern. There are no restrictions in this regard; patterns or charts do not appear to have a use-by date, a time when they expire. In the practice of astrology, charts are immortal. They are receptacles of variations of a pattern carried into new generations, like myths carried by culture through literature as well as through people's lives and people's stories. Charts are patterns - patterns are people - people are stories - stories are patterns - patterns are charts.

Family horoscopes

Astrologers accept that members of the same family will all have natal charts which display variations of a pattern. In the same manner that family members will examine a new born child to see if he or she has their father's eyes or mother's nose, the astrologer looks to see if the infant has "the family chart", the family pattern, the family mark. Like our woven cloth on the loom, the family's strange attractors draw unto themselves particular "colours and shapes" that ensure the continuation of its overall pattern. The very idea of family patterns, whether astrological or psychological, is an exercise in "living" fractal geometry.

We can see a simple family pattern active in the British royal family. Queen Elizabeth II, born in 1926, has her natal Venus at 13^0 57' Pisces. Her first born child, Prince Charles, born in 1948, was born when Venus was at 16^0 Libra. The two zodiac positions of Venus are separated by what astrologers call a bi-quintile (two times the aspect of 72^0 which is one fifth of a circle). Later in 1961, Diana Spencer was born when Venus was at 24^0 Taurus - a position which is both quintile the Queen's Venus as well as two quintiles from Charles'. A simple pattern was being formed (*see figure 13*). Diana marries Charles and their first born child, William (1982), has his natal Venus in the same place in the zodiac as his mother – 24^0 to 25^0 Taurus. Their second born child, Harry (1984), has his natal Venus located at the same place in the zodiac as his father - 16^0 to 17^0 Libra.

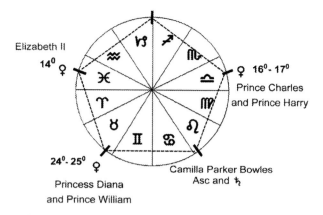

Figure 13 – A family pattern within the British royal family of Venus in a 5th harmonic (quintile, 72°) relationship between a grandmother (Elizabeth II), her son (Charles), his wife and their two sons. Charles' second wife and step mother to William and Harry has her Ascendant and Saturn in the Leo position of the pattern. (Research by *Jigsaw*.)

Camilla Parker Bowles, who was always in the background of the relationship, not surprisingly fits into this pattern with her Ascendant and Saturn in early degrees of Leo and, not surprisingly, this early Leo position was filled by the great grandmother of the family, Queen Elizabeth, The Queen Mother, who had her MC in this position. The empty slot in the pattern in early Capricorn could easily have been filled by the horoscope of a beloved dog or horse, for these patterns are not anthropocentric. In this family "fractal", Camilla's marriage to Charles in 2005 allowed her chart to officially fill the space created when the Queen Mother died in 2002. In a linear dynamic world, the odds of this pattern forming are about 1 in 60 million. However, this is the *non-linear* dynamic world where it has been discovered that patterns will be self-organising and emerge quite naturally and therefore such odds are meaningless. There are many other patterns in this family in the same way that there are many patterns in every family and every group. Furthermore, all of these patterns are self-organising and seek to "fill" themselves by drawing other charts and moments of time into their basins.

Lock-in, a planet becomes linked to a meaning

The existence of these emergent and self-organising patterns in astrology is not proof of astrology but is instead proof of the presence of the chaotic paradigm. However, the fact that astrologers recognize these patterns means that they have, over thousands of years, assigned them meaning. Over time as a pattern grows and spreads through a culture, it would eventually acquire what is known in complexity as "lock-in": the condition that occurs when a particular expression of an idea, object or pattern has become so dominant in the culture that it becomes resistant to change, and acquires homeostatic qualities. Thus, for example, Venus around 3,500 B.C.E., may well have began to absorb symbols and meanings through a tribal family (as in the case of the British royal family), and slowly a tribal and cultural self-organising pattern emerges. Then by blending with different cultures over time, these patterns and their assigned astrological meaning would change but eventually, according to complexity science, they acquire lock-in. Thus the astrological meanings of the planets are co-created by a culture's engagement with the self-organising and naturally emergent astrological patterns.

Grand aspect patterns

Astrologers acknowledge that when certain aspects within a natal horoscope form a particular geometrical shape, such as a grand trine (three planets in an equilateral triangle) or a grand cross (four planets in a square), that patterns will have meaning beyond the individual planets/houses/signs combinations. Termed grand aspect patterns, such patterns are viewed as particular signature shapes, like images within a fractal, and these patterns are expected to be reflected in a self-similar manner in other family charts of past and future generations.

The astrologer will also consider an incomplete natal grand aspect pattern as possessing a teleological quality, like an attractor, which seeks its own completion by drawing people and events into the person's life. Additionally, astrologers use this idea of pattern not only in an individual's chart but also across history. In a collection of historical charts, let us say of leaders of a nation, if there is a vacant space in a collective pattern of their charts, the expectation is that the pattern will draw in a new leader which will complete or add to the pattern.

An example of this can be seen in the pattern of the death of leaders that links the execution of Charles I of England (1649) with the natal chart of Louis XVI of France, executed in 1793, and then with the natal chart of Abraham Lincoln who was born on 12 February 1809 with a Jupiter-Pluto conjunction in the middle degrees of Pisces which formed a square to the Pluto axis created by the two executed kings (*see figure 14*).

Since Abraham Lincoln's assassination there have been a further three US presidents assassinated: James Garfield born (born 19 November 1831) assassinated in 1881, William McKinley (born 29 January 1843) assassinated in 1901, and John F Kennedy (born 29 May 1917) assassinated in 1963. All of them have their Jupiter/Pluto midpoints involved in this growing grand cross. The empty space at the middle degrees of Virgo waits for another assassination or perhaps it has already been filled by a previous death.

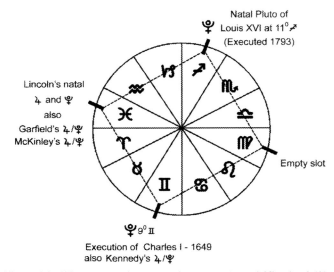

Figure 14 - The pattern between the execution of Charles I (England) and its links to the natal horoscopes of Louis XVI of France and all four assassinated US presidents. (Research by Jigsaw.)

Regardless of the meaning of this pattern of executions and assassinations, it is another example of the self-organising and emergent patterns that astrologers map. Additionally it is also an example of how astrologers work with history and cycles, moving across countries and across time. Astrologers recognize that the pattern itself has power and motivation, but with the understandings of chaos theory we no longer need some divine hand producing these patterns. They are the natural expression of a non-linear dynamic system. In this way aspect patterns can be considered a form of attractor, the heart beating in a pattern drawing into itself, in this case over hundreds of years, the correct components for its shape and meaning.

We can also see, once again, a way in which such an attractor can be instrumental in shaping and eventually producing lock-in of the symbolic meaning of a planetary combination across cultures and history within the astrological corpus.

Neither science, nor religion - insights on the nature of astrology

Astrology has generally, over its history, proven resistant to reductionist approaches. In 1967, before the public knowledge of chaos theory, when astrologer and philosopher Dane Rudhyar[13] talked of the horoscope as a complex structure which is reflective of relationships and which, therefore, cannot be broken down to its parts, most astrologers agreed with him. Chaos theory and chaotic psychology would also agree, for whether astrology is valid or not, its practice endeavours to map patterns that give information about the quality of a life or an object in a relationship-rich environment. Such systems are now known to be non-linear and as astrology was co-created by humanity in dialogue with the heavens it is logical that it, too, is a complex system unresponsive to reductionism. So astrology is unable to respond to the experimental methods of the linear dynamic world as it cannot yield consistently to statistical methods, nor can it be replicated in the laboratory setting, or indeed in any setting. Self-similarity is *not* the same as duplication.

Nor, chaotically thinking, can it seek a place within artisan god-based religions, steered by some divine external hand, for the spontaneous emergence of patterns and order from the void does not require, nor have any place for a cosmic order.

Astrology is a unique hybrid between the linear world and the non-linear as it uses the predictable Newtonian clockwork solar system as its pattern-sensitive pallet to understand the emerging patterns of the living world. No other tool or practice[14] straddles and joins the two worlds, for science sits firmly in one while divination sits firmly in the other.

[13] D. Rudhyar. *The Lunation Cycle*.
[14] Alchemy may have once also held this unique position, being a mixture of chemistry and a divine quest but it was not used as a predictive tool.

In this unique position the practice of astrology is not dependant on the presence of a divine force, but if one is present then it suggests a divine which is immanent, pluralist and omnipresent and at the same time, unlike an artisan God, is non-transcendent, non-formed and non-hierarchical, as it grants no special privileges to humans or any other life force or object. It is All-Not-Knowing rather than the All Knowing deity or deities of divination and is filled with the overwhelming intent and desire for the creation of order, an order which is being continually co-created by the super-rich interplay between life, all of the biosphere, and with itself.

In summary, then, to an astrologer thinking within the chaotic paradigm, astrology is no more than but also no less than a emergent tool, created by humanity and the heavens which can be employed to help a person navigate through the unfolding "fractals" of their life.

Chaos - mathematical findings	Common practices of astrologers
Sensitive Dependence on Initial Conditions (SDIC). Initial conditions dictate the unfolding patterns.	The moment of birth will influence the unfolding pattern of a person's life. The horoscope.
Phase Portraits – an image of the attractors, basins and flexibility of a pattern which can be used to predict the times and qualities of changes to the pattern.	The creation of a horoscope which can be used to observe the unfolding patterns and timing of these patterns in a person's life.
Strange Attractors – the moving foci which seems to invisibly influence the external events or pattern.	Planetary/zodiacal combinations which define the nature or quality of what the person will attract towards themselves and the story of their life.
Hopf Bifurcation – a change in the pattern which can lead to new patterns or entropic chaos – death.	A time in a person's life indicated by a predictive catalyst where the individual can be encouraged to take the path which yields the most creative options.
Saddle Points – the point where bifurcations occur.	Sensitive points in the horoscope which, when receiving some form of predictive catalyst, will result in events of a certain quality occurring in the person's life.
Self-similarity and scale invariance. Repeating themes in patterns which occur in unrelated systems – e.g. river systems and the bronchi of lungs.	Astrologers' use of cycles which link planetary cycles with smaller cycles within an individual's (or country's or organisation's) life.
Homeostasis – the ability that a system has to resist change.	The astrological method of grading the potential of predictive events with regards to its ability to indicate change in the person's life.
Lock-in – a pattern becoming resist to change.	The symbolic meaning of planet evolving and then maintaining a level of consistency over time.

Figure 15 – Some of the possible links between the findings of chaos theory and the practice of astrology. This table does not attempt to be exhaustive but simply to summarise the most obvious parallels that have been discussed in this chapter.

5

LIVING INSIDE A FRACTAL

'Tis all a chequer-board of nights and days
Where Destiny with Men for pieces plays:
Hither and thither moves, and mates, and slays,
And one by one back in the closet lays.

The Rubáiyát of Omar Khayyám (1859) st. 49

Our personal experience of life is different to what we are taught by the causal mechanical world. The causal world informs us that all life is meaningless, that having evolved by chance, life is nothing more than an accident of biochemistry and that in accepting the nihilism of this soulless creation we live our insignificant lives, and will one day cease to exist. Any sense of meaning or inner purpose to our lives or the life of any individual is thus a delusion.

However, we know that our experienced internal reality is different, and that many of us do feel a sense of purpose. This difference between our felt experience of life and what we are actually taught about life creates a chasm or a crack which a lot of us fill with the putty of spirituality, religion or personal beliefs. Astrology also steps into this crevasse by emphasising patterns and acknowledging that we have a place in the world, a personal relationship with the heavens and a home in the universe. It thus bestows upon us a sense of belonging and a sense of purpose, undoubtedly contributing to astrology's robust nature within our culture.

Fractals and Fate

In accepting that people feel a sense of purpose in life, astrologers believe that they are able to read some information about this purpose from a birth chart and thus they are actually acknowledging that something is "written" in that chart. By creating a map of the ever-changing but predictable sky for the moment that a person is born and then using this map to talk of the person's journey through life, the astrologer is accepting the presence of some form of fate or destiny. Additionally, as one acknowledges the existence of fate, so one also creates the need for its counter-balance of freewill - that which is not dictated by fate.

The question of what is, and what is not written for a life lies at the heart of astrology, as one can only read what is destined for an individual, freewill by definition being unreadable. Indeed how an astrologer sees this balance between freewill and fate will have a vast impact on the information that he or she considers is contained within the chart and consequently a vast impact on the type of astrology he or she will undertake.

Humanity has long debated these questions of fate and freewill and many wise people have added profound thoughts over the last two and a half thousand years. In fact, the mere weight and sagacious nature of the philosophical arguments around the question of fate and freewill have almost created a block to the debate cascading into other disciplines. Yet despite this, a contemporary voice is that of theoretical physicist Paul Davies. In his concern about the erosion of freewill by the determinism of science, Davies suggests that we do have freewill and defines it as our soul, suggesting that we experience it as a "folk psychology" which exists inside all of us as "a self, a conscious agent who both observes the world and makes decisions"[1]. Thus Davies locates our soul within the confines of our freewill, yet chaos thinking would suggest that Davies' idea of soul may be flawed, not in suggesting its actual presence but rather in defining it as the individual's freewill.

Taking fractals personally

Since Newton, human-kind has held itself separate to the world, seeing all of life as inter-linked but at the same time considering itself to be an elite animal, god-like and separate. Yet the simple and at the same time profound fact is that you are a full member of the biosphere and you live in a cyclic relationship with the void. This is reflected in many ways in your daily life but perhaps one of the most obvious expressions of the void is the need for sleep. The causal world finds the requirement for sleep mysterious, but it can be understood as a nightly need to return to the void to be refreshed. A state where dreams are either the old order being reabsorbed into the void or new order emerging from the void.

Chaos theory and complexity can inform us about life, its emergent pattern-making, self-similar, repeating tenacity. It suggests that by living in relationship to the void we live inside a fractal-like place and if we had a way of plotting our life graphically using a moving pencil, chaos informs us that this moving pencil would not produce random scribble, it would be pulled in certain directions. It may slip into basins - indents in the surface – around which it may then orbit for some time, yet at some time in the future it may glide into fresh areas only to be pulled towards further basins. Remember also that you are not alone. There are other pencils, other entities – not all human and not necessarily all living - which weave in and out of your patterns, blending their patterns with yours in a complex picture.

[1] Paul Davies. (2004) "Undermining Free Will" in *Foreign Policy*. Sep/Oct. Issue 144 :36.

This may seem a strange metaphor for describing a person's life, but is it? If I suggested to you that this imagined pencil drew nothing but random dots and dashes or meaningless scrawl when tracing out your life (the Newtonian world view), how would you feel? Since we already carry a sense that our life is in the process of fulfilling a larger pattern, to be told that it is merely scribble offends our internal reality. Chaotic thinking shows that the way in which a living system unfolds over time is not random. Our life-pencil does produce patterns.

Furthermore, these patterns are not randomly selected. Since a pattern is directed by its strange attractors, the pattern is inherently contained within the system itself, for the pathways open to any living system at times of change are not infinite. The moving pencil of your life is loyal to producing your particular pattern, thus your choices in life will be restricted, influenced or pulled so that they fall within the limits of your pattern. These limits may be quite broad, allowing you a lot of personal choice, but they are there in the same manner as an astrologer sees the limitations imposed by the quality of a planetary combination in a horoscope.

This point is discussed by chaotic psychologists Middleton, Fireman and Di Bello[2] who, in talking about human behaviour, suggested that whilst the exact behaviour of a person is unpredictable from moment to moment, their behaviour remains within the loose boundaries of the strange attractors in their life and consequently the person's ability to freely act in any manner is curtailed by the limits of their unfolding pattern. Any living system, which includes an individual person, only has a finite number of choices which

---

[2] C. Middleton, G. Fireman, R. Di Bello. (1991). "Personality traits as strange attractors". Paper presented at the *Inaugural Meeting for the Society for Chaos Theory in Psychology*. San Fransicso, CA: 19.
http://www.societyforchaostheory.org/ Accessed 15 January, 2004.

are defined by the nature of the strange attractors present in their life.

Similarly philosophical biologists Maturana and Varela[3] , in their more abstract discussion on predicting the outcomes at bifurcation points (points of change), also focus on this balance between the nature of a pattern and its "freewill" to make choices:

> When a living system reaches a bifurcation point, its history of structural coupling will determine the new pathways that become available, but which pathway the system will take remains unpredictable.

The history of structural coupling referred to by Maturana and Varela is the information required to determine the nature of the strange attractors which shape the pathways. Once found, these strange attractors indicate the type of pathways that are presented to the living systems and, by analogy, presented to the human life.

However, in order to expand on this idea of an immanent or inherent quality within a living system, we need to return to the work of Benoit Mandelbrot and fractal geometry. To repeat: the geometry of fractals reveals, in a simple manner, the way in which complex systems behave as they evolve through time. We can link the repeating patterns of a fractal with the repeating themes which occur in the life of an individual or a society across time and across scale and such a link will give us insights into the "moving pencil" of our own lives.

Fractals display an inherent quality for, as a fractal unfolds at any given point, it is unpredictable yet when viewed as a whole, it displays a pattern or shape. Since fractals are closed systems, we can alter the types of pattern through small

---

[3] Humberto Maturana, Varela Francisco. (1987). *The Tree of Knowledge.* Boston: Shambhala: 95.

adjustments to the original formula. So the formula of the fractal is like a seed which contains within it a potential for the final shape.

Look at the fractal mountain scenes in *figure 16*. The seed formulae used to create the fractal landscapes will keep producing, over continual generations, a "mountain scape" or a "cloudy sky". Now precisely how an individual mountain will grow cannot be predicted but what can be predicted is that the fractal will grow within a certain nature or quality as defined by the seed formula. The mountain range on the left in *figure 16* is more rugged and of a different nature to the mountain range on the right because it is produced by a different seed equation. Furthermore, no matter how long we run the equation for the mountain range on the left of the figure, we will continue to produce rugged mountains which will maintain the overall pattern of a rugged mountain range.

Figure 16 - Two fractal landscapes which are images made by taking a formula and feeding its results back into itself – iteration. The two different landscapes were produced by using different seed formulae to create firstly, the mountains and then secondly, another seed formula for the clouds[4]. Each image is thus two fractal seed formulae. However, each image has a particular type of mountain and a particular type of cloud. Further iterations of the seed equations will simply produce more mountains or clouds within the types already present.

[4] Fractal landscapes from http://ata-tenui.ifrance.com Accessed 26 March, 2006.

As the equation is iterated (repeated and therefore moved through time) it will reach key points (saddle points) where it has a finite choice (a bifurcation) as to which path it takes, thus yielding variations within its type of mountain. The timing as to *when* the choices will be presented to the equation and also the *nature* of the choices available for the equation is inherently contained within the actual equation itself. The equation, therefore, has a potential which is rich and varied, like the two different landscapes in *figure 16*, but is still tightly defined by the parameters set by the seed equation. In these fractals, the seed formula contains, or produces, the "fate" of the two different mountain ranges. Its destiny and therefore its fate is to be a particular type of mountain range but the exact shape of each individual mountain or valley is defined by the "freewill" choices at the saddle points.

Astrologers are comfortable with the chaotic under-standing of an inherent quality and the resulting finite choices this quality imposes within a system. Astrologers generally consider that an exact event is unpredictable but that the resulting event is expected to unfold within certain boundaries[5]. Thus predictive work tends to focus on the timing and the quality of the moment. The possible choices open to the client are defined by the boundaries of the indicated planetary/zodiacal configurations.

We know, however, that life is not a just a simple fractal, it-eration following iteration with no unexpected events, yet we are also aware that life has a strong desire for homeostasis. Thus most of us live our lives as part fractal and part complex system, a hybrid of predictability, deterministic patterns and non-predictable emergent new patterns. When your life is run-ning its normal daily and annual patterns you are living within

[5]   Liz Greene. (1996). *The Art of Stealing Fire*. London, UK: CPA Press:147.

your own fractal-like space unfolding the same types of patterns, expecting the same type of events, and containing a certain predictability to your life. Our natural desire for homeostasis continually moves us into such a fractal-like space. Periodically, however, we reach a tipping point (complexity's term for change) or hopf bifurcation (chaos' term for change) which can be a small or large event which results in a change to our whole life and produces brand new patterns and brand new ways of living, when the pencil of our life begins to draw a new type of pattern. Quickly, however, we seek a return to homeostasis and the new pattern achieves lock-in. This then becomes the new theme of our life until the next tipping point. An example of our need for homeostasis is revealed when we move home: the first thing most people do is get one room organised in order to get some normal routine running; or after a shock event, the first thing people do is try and get some "normalness" happening in their life again.

Astrologers are also comfortable with the chaotic thinking that there are only certain times when a life is open to new patterns. Indicators like a secondary progressed Sun changing sign would be a marker of such a time where the event could be subtle and tiny yet still lead to huge repercussions. Indicators like a major transit could be a bifurcation or tipping point where the event was larger and more noticeable, also leading to great change of lifestyle with new order emerging. This idea is reflected in the astrological work of many authors and summed up in the words of Dane Rudhyar when he refers to his astrological approach to predictive work[6]:

> Events cannot be foretold accurately, but the
> conditions needed by an individual if he is to grow
> to his full stature as an individual can be pre-
> diagnosed. The astrologer can discover from the

---

[6] D. Rudhyar. *The Lunation Cycle*: 104.

progressions the main turning points in the life of a
person.

In chaos theory it is the strange attractor which shapes the
quality and which sets the limits of the options open for choice;
within astrology it is the planetary combinations. We can begin to see that chaos theory can indeed comment on the
philosophical notions of fate and freewill by drawing on its
discovery of the immanent quality and finite choices contained
with the patterns of life, and thus contained within a human
life. Yet everywhere we turn in exploring the immanent nature of patterns, be they in Mandelbrot's geometry or in chaotic
psychology, we are pulled towards this idea of a strange
attractor.

Living with strange sttractors

The strange attractor, as already discussed in Chapter Three,
is central to the idea that spontaneous new patterns emerge
on "the edge of chaos", and although their formation is still
not fully understood, they do define the nature of the patterns.
A person's life may at first appear to have no order and no
reason for unfolding events. Neither an observer nor the
individual themselves may actually have conscious knowledge
of the presence of a strange attractor, yet as time passes and by
observing the events from a particular perspective, an order
will be observed. Indeed this is used in a simplistic manner as
the instrument of all mystery novels and films: in the beginning
all is confusion and there is no order; then we are given a
series of clues and eventually a pattern is revealed. However,
when we personally experience such revelations in our own
life - a meaningless event like a missed bus which yields a new
pathway that makes sense of our lives many years later – we
think that such an event was not a fluke but rather directed
by an unseen hand. When we encounter these patterns, our

mental predisposition to the doctrines of the linear world is such that we tend to seek metaphysical or divine explanations for them.

Jungian psychologist James Hillman[7] uses this type of experience as proof of the concept of the human soul. He suggests that our soul is like an external entity that knows our fate or destiny and leads us to that place. One may call it the personal daemon or the dharma of the person's life, or simply the will of God, or the gods. Chaos theory, however, would either call it the seed equation of a fractal or the strange attractor within a complex living system and even though it is within the system, we experience it as an external force. For as we orbit around its basin it seems very much as Hillman suggests: an external force directing our life to an end of which we are unsure but which becomes clear once achieved; a pulling towards a defined pattern which is only known and understood once it is complete.

Indeed our personal internal experience of the workings of the strange attractors in our life leads us to a sense of our own soul, the personal journey which seems to know the path that makes sense of our lives. Davies says that the human soul lies in our free will; Hillman suggests that the human soul is external to us and guides us through our lives; chaos indicates that the human soul is our personal way of articulating our experience of the immanent nature of the pattern in which we live.

Serendipity, synchronicity and strange attractors
Yet not all of the revealed patterns in a person's life are involved in that person's own great narrative. As we move through life we encounter other strange attractors and emerging patterns

---

[7] James Hillman. (1996). *The Soul's Code, In Search of Character and Calling.* Sydney, Australia: Random House.

and such new patterns may grow and become important for us while others simply fade away. Indeed the findings of both chaos and complexity propose that the more interlinked we are with our environment, the more we will see the emergence of new patterns. These patterns are generated by strange attractors. If these new patterns appear to have no significance in our life, we label them "serendipity"; if they also have a link to some internal image, dream or fantasy we may even label them "synchronicity". Regardless of whether they are deeply symbolic to us or seen as simply odd patterns, their presence in our life always fills us with a sense of awe and mystery.

In October, 2004, I received this email from one of my astrology students, an example of her encounter with a strange attractor and the wonder that it produced in her mind:

> For your interest I had my last of five sweeps of Pluto over my 12th house Saturn on 4th October. What a week that was. The weekend before I met a lot of my family I hadn't seen for twenty five years due to death of my Scorpio uncle, generally a good day - he had a very good and timely death...
>
> ... On the 4th [of the month] I heard of my friend Karen's (another Scorpio) son's death and have been spending a lot of time with her. I have just talked to another friend today who has terminal cancer (he has known this for over a year) and he is also a Scorpio and apart from his own illness he is at present in a hospice watching his twelve year old son, Max, die from a brain tumor that he only found out about a few days ago [around the 6th of the month]. My friend Karen and Max's mum (yet again another Scorpio) were both born on 25th October, the same day as my on and off again partner, 25th October, so clearly I have a link to this date. Max's father, my friend who is dying of cancer, was also

born on the 28th October (another late October and Scorpio date).

There seems to be some awful pattern in all this pain in people I love. The odds are against randomness but I don't understand - I don't expect you to either - I thought you may be interested purely astrologically.

Anyway life remains a massive mystery; all seems to point to the necessity of cherishing it[8].

The student has been swept into the basin of a "number" strange attractor which collected unto itself instances of the number "2" and the number "5" (or late October date) and combined them both with emotionally painful situations. The end result was that she sensed that she was encountering a divine pattern, or place of purpose which had its own "life" and which existed beyond her worldly vision.

The student, raised in the linear belief that all possible outcomes have the same chance of occurrence, recognized the impossible odds that this pattern could randomly form. Yet the pattern *was* present and according to the logic of the statistical linear world it was so unlikely that its very presence assumed a mysterious nature.

Here is another strange attractor story retold by the mathematician Warren Weaver[9]

A church choir in Beatrice, Nebraska, made up of fifteen members was due to begin their practice at 7.30 pm and choir members were expected to arrive ten minutes early to be ready and in voice for the practice. But on 1st of March 1950 all fifteen members were late. They were late for a variety of ordinary reasons. One girl stayed back to finish her

---

[8] Personal email and quoted with permission.
[9] Warren Weaver.(1963). *Lady Luck, the Theory of Probability.* Harmondsworth, UK: Pelican Books.

geometry assignment, another two wanted to listen
to the end of a particularly exciting program, the
minister's wife delayed him and his daughter because
she was ironing the daughter's dress, another
member had to be woken from a nap and was slow
to stir. The reasons went on and all were ordinary
excuses, and there were ten separate sets of excuses.
But it was just as well as that evening at 7.25 pm,
when the choir was meant to be picking up their
hymn books for rehearsal the building blew up and
was completely destroyed.

Weaver calculated the odds against the entire choir being late
on this particular night at one chance in a million. This may
be the case but I wonder what the mathematical odds would
be if he also added in the chance that the local church would
explode - a not too frequent event. I am sure that the figure
would be substantially higher than one in a million. Yet if you
think of this story not within the linear world of statistics and
probabilities (where all options are infinite and all have an
equal chance) but rather within the non-linear world of chaos,
then the fifteen people, all in a relationship via their
community, are all involved in a collective unfolding pattern
with the church building. The choir and the church are
connected in a pattern which is focused around the celebration
of a religion through the act of singing, but this pattern has
clearly reached a bifurcation and the choices now open to the
church building and the choir contain a finite two options:
the choice for the church is to explode or not to explode, the
choice for the choir *as a group* is to be killed or not be killed.

However, the story tells us more. The fifteen people must
also have had some type of social contact other than just their
role as choir members. This other pattern clearly did not
contain the death of only one member of the group, so the
option was that either they must all die or all live. Thus all of

them had to be late to avoid the explosion. This may seem an odd way to look at this story but chaos theory is opening up this type of non-linear thinking: regardless of whether the event happened in the linear world – which would label these events a fluke – or in the non-linear world, the experience for all fifteen people, and indeed for the whole township, would have been one of awe and mystery and a sense of an encounter with a divine hand.

Notice, however, in the non-linear appraisal of this story, how the church building is given agency in the same manner as the people in the choir. This is an example of the non-anthropocentric nature of the chaotic world.

4 North Parade Passage, Bath, England

Here is another place story indicating agency. This is the story of a young French refugee who arrived in England in the 1680s. She was a baker by trade and it is thought that her name was Sally Lunn[10], although this could have been the name of her special cakes called "soleil et lune" – the sun and moon. Fleeing the horrors of the persecution of the Huguenots, she decided, for reasons unknown, to settle in the English town of Bath. Here she baked her cakes. Her special buns were a huge success and while others tried hard to copy them, her skill with the rich, soft and delicate dough inspired customers to specifically request the Sally Lunn bun. The story goes that after some time, Sally settled into a house at 4 North Parade Passage, now considered the oldest house in Bath, and took her secret bun recipe with her. This house became home to her bakery and has done so now for over three hundred years. To this day you can go to her house and partake of one of her famous buns. The secret recipe is linked to the title of the house, so

---

[10] Sally Lunn's House http://www.sallylunns.co.uk/new_web_site/All_Sally_web_pages/UntitledFrameset-5.htm Accessed 23 January, 2004.

whoever owns the house gains the recipe. The house and the world famous Sally Lunn bun are linked in a pattern.

And here the story could have ended except for one interesting twist. Archeologists recently discovered that the house was built on the remains of a 12ᵗʰ century bakery used by the monks of the Bath Abbey. What was more startling was that below those foundations it was found that the monks had built their bakery over a Roman bakery dating from the period 100 to 500 C.E. For nearly 2,000 years this small patch of ground on the road to the hot springs at Bath had either been a bakery or a place wishing to be a bakery. Here was a location spinning a pattern written in flour and yeast.

Whose story and whose pattern is the dominant theme here: the French baker, Sally Lunn, fleeing the slaughter of the Huguenots who happens to find herself, by a fluke of ships and available passage, in the town of Bath or the strange attractor of place, with bread as its signature pattern, now known as 4 North Parade Passage? In this story both the physical place and Sally Lunn have agency and both have their own patterns but now we see how these patterns of place and person combine to bring both success: the place fulfils its "desire" to be a bakery, the baker fulfils his or her "desire" to make bread, and as these patterns of place and person merge, the result is a flourishing patisserie.

Strange attractors can be a place, a person, an idea, a painting, an animal, a piece of music, a story, or the like. There is no hierarchy in chaotic systems and humans are just one voice, one unit in the web of life, neither in the centre nor in a higher position.

If we had asked Sally Lunn in her old age how she had managed to arrive at the idea of settling in Bath, she would probably have answered that she felt drawn to the location, for this is a very human feeling which most of us experience and to which we respond at different times in our lives. Indeed this feeling of being drawn towards an unknown pattern which only has meaning after we have done all the right things was actually first defined by Aristotle in the 4th century B.C.E.

Teleology – seeing the work of a strange attractor

Aristotle put forward a theory for understanding the world. He rejected the teachings of Heraclitus (c. 535 - 475 B.C.E.) whose philosophy as we have already seen contained some of the early thinking in chaos theory, and suggested that there were four fundamental causes which bring something into existence. The first three of his causes were concerned with the physical material of an object its shape and its shaper: a wooden table is grown from wood, (the physical material) hewn into a table (its shape) by a carpenter (its shaper). In these first three causes Aristotle described the linear world of objects, but he added a fourth cause, the *causa finalis*, which he defined as the desire of the wood to become a table or the desire of clay to become a bowl. This desire of matter to seek its final form is called *telos* (discussed in Chapter Two). It is the idea that matter seeks its own order[11] and thus the emerging patterns from the chaotic void do not just randomly unfold but unfold with order and with purpose. Indeed it would seem that Aristotle was referring to both the linear and the non-linear worlds, for his first three causes focused on pushing something into being in a causal manner whilst his final cause is suggestive of an order which pulls the system towards its desired end. The clay seeks to become a bowl and therefore the concept of "bowl" becomes the active element and pulls the clay and the potter together to achieve the final result. Using the idea of *telos* one could suggest, for example, that the bakery in Bath was a location which desired to be a place of baking and so pulled towards itself not only the Roman bakers of 100 C.E.

---

[11] J.V. Luce. *An Introduction to Greek Philosophy*: 118.

but later Christian monks and Sally Lunn. *Telos* is order created from *within* the system.

Over time *telos* has been given many different definitions and although denied by the linear world, it has refused to slip into the oblivion of history. Thus apart from philosophical *telos* (Aristotle's version) and dualistic *telos* (also known as theological *telos* and used to support the belief in God who has planned the universe), there is also process teleology (the idea that creation or evolution is guided, not from an external deity but from an inherent unfolding within the creature or object that is evolving[12]), cosmic teleology (which seems to be a recent return to Aristotle's idea that all things are pulled towards a sense of their completion and perfection[13]) and even more recently ethical *telos* (which has emerged in the UK to protect pigs from being genetically modified on the grounds that the animal has a right to develop towards its "essential nature"[14]). Regardless of its many definitions, *telos* is the concept that we are pulled towards a predefined end which can also be described as the action of entering the basin of a strange attractor within a system. Thus the principle of *telos* may well be Aristotle's empirical understanding of the experience of living in a relationship-rich world and encountering strange attractors.

If *telos* is the general principle of being pulled through a pattern-making life, then we could say our souls are the

---

[12]   Arthur Young. (1976). *The Reflexive Universe: Evolution of Consciousness.* New York: Delacorte Press.

[13]   Anthony Mansueto.(1998). "Cosmic Teleology and the Crisis of the Sciences" in *Philosophy of Science.* on-line Journal of papers presented for the Twentieth World Congress of Philosophy, in Boston, Massachusetts 10 August, 1998. http://www.bu.edu/wcp/Papers/Scie/ScieMans.htm Accessed 16 October, 2004.

[14]   Michael Hauskeller. (2005). "Telos:The Revival of an Aristotelian Concept in Present Day Ethics." In the *Inquiry*, February, 2005; 48(1): 62-75.

personal experience of being pulled by *telos* into a meaningful existence. This recognises the notion of "soul" as our personal understanding of our role within the pattern, our contribution to the pattern of our life which in turn adds to the pattern of our family's life which in turn adds to the pattern of our community's life, not just within our own time but over thousands of generations. Also, in this model, our destiny is the pattern itself and our fate is to be born into a particular landscape of strange attractors.

However, as implied in the story of Sally Lunn, or the church in Beatrice, Nebraska, we are not always the centre of our own stories or if we are, our stories are blended with other non-human stories; and in the same way as a location or a place can have agency or influence, so too can a culture. In fact, cultures contain extremely powerful strange attractors that can propel a nation to war or rebellion or a people into patriotism and loyalty. These collective cultural patterns are found in music (patterns in sounds), as well as in myths and stories (patterns in words).

Myths and Patterns

Myths are special stories which have acquired "lock-in" in our culture. They probably began as stories which focused on a reoccurring theme over many generations. Some of these narratives were about natural phenomena but many were and still are about human behaviour, human attitudes and human characteristics. These stories are verbal fractals as they reproduce themselves over time in a self-similarity manner. Such a reproducing narrative may also spread itself over different cultures and through different periods of history, until slowly it achieves lock-in and is labelled as mythology.

Myths are an unexplained curiosity to the causal linear world, expressed by Robert Segal when he says:

> Each discipline harbours multiple theories of myth.
> Strictly, theories of myth are theories of some much
> larger domain, with myth a mere subset. For
> example, anthropological theories of myth are
> theories of culture *applied* to the case of myth.
> Psychological theories of myth are theories of the
> mind. Sociological theories of myth are theories of
> society. There are no theories of myth itself …
> There is no study of myth as myth[15].

Segal defines myth as a meaningful story which features the life of gods. Yet in the chaotic, non-linear world view, myth is the verbal expression of a reoccurring pattern. If a story is localized to a small community, we call it a folk story or fairy tale. If it is a story with a lesson or moral, we call it a fable or a parable. If it seems to have symbolic meaning for many people with plots and themes, we call it a myth. The myths may be full of advice or warnings about what pathways to take when we meet certain cultural bifurcation points, or they may be the "blueprints" of different types of human profiles, immortally preserved outside the gene pool. The important point is that the information myths carry is perpetuated in a fractal-like manner[16]. As we retell these stories over and over again, weaving in and out of many generations, the stories alter, appear in other stories, and over time reshape themselves to once again resemble the original story pattern[17]. The Celtic story of Rhiannon and the gold cup becomes the story of Arthur and the quest for the Holy Gail, which becomes the story of Luke Sky Walker in Star Wars, and on and on and on…

In the chaotic world our cultural myths are like living beings, with the same "power" and the same teleological desires

---

[15] Robert Segal. (2004). *Myth, A very Short Introduction*. Oxford, UK: Oxford University Press:2.

[16] J.van Eenwyk. *Archetypes and Strange Attractors*: 67.

[17] see , J.F. Bierlein.(1994). *Parallel Myths*. New York: Ballantine Books.

to seek their perfect form. Indeed, given their immortality and their distilled nature, chaotic thinking can remove myths from the linear-world's derogatory category of superstition, silly wives tales and meaningless fairy stories and place them in a new position. This new position implies that myths are verbal blueprints of human life-patterns which help to maintain human life, just as human life helps to maintain them. We and our myths co-create each other.

A question of charisma and fractals

We know that by following the geometry of a fractal, zooming in deeper and deeper, generation after generation, that the image of the whole fractal will once again emerge unexpectedly from the order and the unfolding pattern, slightly different than the original but clearly recognisable. As we move deeper and deeper into the famous m-set, for example, we find new little Buddha-shaped images, and if we zoom in on one of these new images, moving forward for an infinite number of generations, we will find, periodically, newer, slightly different but complete m-sets (*see figure 6 and 7 in Chapter Three*). This holds true for all fractals and we can suggest that it holds true for all living systems.

This principal can give us a unique understanding of great charismatic or mythic figures in history: Napoleon, Alexander the Great and Joan of Arc, for example, were able to unleash great forces in the collective and carve new paths in history, while great creators such as Beethoven, Mozart or van Gogh seem to be able to reflect back to us something that we deeply recognise. Powerful figures who bring great change to a country or a culture through their ideas may well reflect back to us a master image of a cultural fractal, and so we respond to their art, their music or their words. Such an individual will not only appear to hold all answers but become the receptor of many different patterns seeking expression. Such an embodiment of the repetition of the main fractal pattern (and we know that in fractals this must occur) would produce a seemingly divine charismatic individual whom Jungian psychologists define as "archetypal" and neo-Platonists consider reflective of the world soul.

But we are not all charismatic figures, so what of the other parts of the fractal?

The Whole within each One, the One within the Whole

If we do live inside a fractal-like space then our own individual life must also contain the seeds or knowledge of the "whole". For just as a charismatic person may outwardly display a focused image of the seed of the complete pattern, all of us contain within the patterns of our own lives the potential of the whole; this is the nature of a fractal. Thus we will instinctively sense that we are part of a larger whole, yet at the same time have an understanding that the whole is also contained within us.

Nevertheless, such a wholeness is not restricted to human life, for it embraces the full diversity of the biosphere, if not beyond. In the chaotic paradigm there is no concept of separateness or outside, nor is there any place or position for an observer, an isolated entity, and there is no distinction between an "us" and a "them" or an "us" and "it". For example, if crop circles are genuine, then in this way of thinking they may be a field singing to its landscape with no regard for human life, yet they also act as an attractor to other life which is drawn towards them by instinctually recognising a common pattern. Humans, as only one such life form, may even actively engage in the culture of "fields who sing to themselves" by reproducing "fake" crop circles in other fields which in turn teaches other fields how to make their own crop circles. So like bees to flowers, humans help the spread of crop circles. In this example, humans are merged with the (possible) culture or desire of the fields to form circles through the mutually sympathetic understanding of patterns. In the chaotic paradigm there is no outside, there is no human life separate to the rest of the biosphere. The wholeness is complete and agency can exist in any part of the system, a description that can be most difficult for us to fully comprehend.

Thus, if the void is the creative source then by extension we are born into a fractal/story and this pattern contains our family and cultural dynamics, as well as our own life. Our fate and our destiny is to live within the parameters of this pattern. Our soul is our personal experience of the teleological forces within the fractal and our freewill exists in the choices we make at the saddle points of our life, choices which are limited by the larger force, the strange attractors of the pattern to which we belong. We may go through tipping points where new order and a new life can emerge but even this new life would be in some way within the quality of our own patterns. However, our sense of uniqueness is justified, for it is the uniqueness connected with any part of a fractal: beautiful, wondrous and rich with order but always the pattern goes on forever, generation after generation after iteration after iteration.

We live, therefore, both in our own part of a fractal, containing the whole, as well as part of that whole that continues. We are a citizen in our own story and a character of many other stories many of which are not even human.

6

WORKING WITH CHAOTIC ASTROLOGY

If we accept that astrology has a place in chaos, then it is valid to explore what astrologers gain by acknowledging and actively encouraging the principles of chaos and complexity into their subject. Such an approach is independent of the type of astrology already being practised, since it asks for a change in the attitude of the astrologer rather than a change in any astrological techniques being used. So, since most clients are seeking new ideas and new opportunities, the first question to ask is: where can the chaotic astrologer find "the edge of chaos"?

Finding the Edge of Chaos

We live inside a system which behaves in a complex manner and as noted before, "the edge of chaos" is not an edge of chaos, an abstract space created in a laboratory bench which implies a place of total break down of all order. The "edge of chaos" is, according to complexity, the place where patterns exist and all new order emerges[1]. This may sound like a simple statement but the word "all" indicates it is profound. Complexity has found that new order *only* emerges in the phase shifts from static to totally chaotic. Therefore finding "the edge of chaos" and knowing how to travel back and forth from this rich creative place is vital. Indeed, if we wish to actively

---

[1] S. Kauffman. *At Home in the Universe: The Search for the Laws of Self-Organization and Complexity*: 15.

generate the environment for new opportunities and new ideas, then we need to look for it within our own lives and the lives of our clients and knowing how to visit this edge must surely be one of life's basic skills. But what and where in your life is this place?

If we look at a person's life or the life of an economy, company or even of a nation then, as discussed in Chapter Three, we know that a life with too little input will fall into a static state. A static life is a life heading towards entropic chaos, the state of slowly losing energy and grinding to a halt. We see this as a person moves into their final stage of life. They may have already moved to a smaller residence and as they get older or frailer, they may eventually move into one of their children's homes or a nursing home. Along the way they will be ridding themselves of the chattels of life. Over time the person becomes smaller in the world and by reducing their networks, they begin to reduce their potential for new order to spontaneously appear. This is a life moving towards entropic chaos. In old age it is accepted and welcomed by the individual. In a younger person we recognise this as a dangerous condition and one which is flirting with an untimely death. In contrast, if a person has too many relationships and too much input, there will be a flood of information to which a person is constantly reacting and they will become stressed. This is the pathway to a breakdown which chaos would see as pushing into infinity, another form of entropic chaos.

So "the edge of chaos" is located in the place between our comfort zone and the place into which we fall in times of total stress when we are overloaded with too many activities and responsibilities. The place between these two states is the place we need to visit in order to enrich our existence. This is "the edge of chaos" which Kauffman[2] calls living between

---

[2] ibid.

structure and surprise, for it requires a balancing act between our routines and order, and the unplanned, the chaotic and the spontaneous, too much movement in either direction and the ideas and options cease. Our daily lives need to contain routine; they also need to contain times of being pushed out of our comfort zones into encounters with new relationships, new ideas and new conversations. It is through these encounters that new patterns are able to enter our lives: these may be new friendships, new opportunities for career moves, or new intellectual or creative insights.

Thus the journey of life is about learning how to keep our connections in balance, just enough to be creative but not so much that we are overloaded and become non-productive. If we can maintain such a balance, then research in chaos and complexity informs us that our life will contain recognisable patterns and cycles, as well as generate new patterns and new order. Some of these will be physiological and will provide a base for good health; others will be in our thinking and creativity; still others in the unfolding events of our lives.

Remember "the edge of chaos" does not have to be a place of great disturbance, it simply has to be a place full of relationships.

In 2004, I was part of the audience at the Cheltenham Literary Festival where the prolific and celebrated English crime writer Ruth Rendell was being interviewed. Rendell was asked if she planned her books before she wrote them. She replied that she did not, that she would start to write the characters and loosely shape their relationships with each other and then suddenly from nowhere "I really have no idea how it happens" a pattern emerges and unfolds "and it turns out right in the end". Rendell is using her "edge of chaos" to write her books. Firstly she drafts her characters, then she establishes feedback loops between these characters and with these relationships in place, she then opens her mind to the emerging patterns that chaos and complexity informs us will occur. The new order that emerges is of course the story line, for the narrative, the plot of the murder mystery, is her form of new order. For Ruth Rendell, the creative source in her life is constantly being enriched with the new characters of her books and from this complex environment new ideas emerge and these new story-lines lead to new books.

For most of us, however, we seek this creative disturbance in other ways. Many people find the daily routine of work and family overpowering with its regularity and for this reason people cram a hobby into their busy daily routines, a hobby which pushes them into new social groups and new activities. Such new activities stir the "Nile silt" of their lives and enable new patterns to emerge. Other people take holidays which are never really designed for physical relaxation but to break up routine, for they push us into unfamiliar territory or unfamiliar daily routines. Holidays are really vacations to "the edge of chaos".

Yet as we visit the "edge of chaos" there is a key point to grasp about the emergence of the new patterns and that is that they will occur in unexpected areas and may appear to be random with no link to the holiday or the hobby. This is the non-linear world, yet it functions with the same surety as causality for new patterns will emerge but there will be a consistent lack of obvious causal links. This makes "the edge of chaos" a most exotic destination as a person may take up a new hobby, shake themselves out of their comfort zone, go and meet new people, learn to cope with a new situation and then suddenly an immoveable issue with an old uncle that has been causing difficulties in their life for years starts to resolve. A woman may take a vacation to a new and strange place and encounter culture shock. A few months later, after years of trying to have children, she may fall pregnant. In the past, society has termed this as a coincidence as the pair of events seem to have no causal link. However, thinking in chaos and complexity indicates that, although the expression of the new order may be unpredictable, rather than being a fluke event, its occurrence is a real certainty. This is a critical point, for by stepping out of your comfort zone in one area of your life, you may well help break stagnation in another.

To the chaotic astrologer the potential of this concept is immense, for by using the tools of natal charts and predictive work, the astrologer may be able to help the person first know the times when it is best to visit "the edge of chaos" and then suggest possible actions to help create or precipitate the desired changes.

Yet, despite the potential this place holds for us in our lives, most of us resist visiting this zone. Some people avoid change outright; others live in too large a network and wonder why they are always stressed but achieve little. Either way the history of a person's willingness to visit "the edge of chaos" forms, over time, what is known as a fitness landscape and understanding these landscapes can be a useful tool for the chaotic astrologer.

At this stage it is tempting to draw the simple conclusions that mutable signs may be prone to being overloaded with information and thus tend to move beyond "the edge of chaos" while a person with an over-abundance of fixed signs in a natal chart could display reluctance to move out of their comfort zone. However, although at times this may be the case, it is more reliable to look at the chart in conjunction with the person's history in order to gauge their ability to live comfortably between structure and surprise.

Fitness Landscapes – The client's history and their needs
Whilst some people and some charts do seem to be born in better starting positions, we all inhabit our own particular landscapes.

When we strive to achieve something, such as a financially viable life, a successful business, or a happy relationship, we are climbing a peak in our fitness landscape. The pinnacle represents our goals. The actual peak that we are climbing describes the decisions we have made regarding the best way to achieve our goals. The peak is limited and grows in steepness and therefore as we head towards the summit, we tend to work harder for less advancement until eventually all we are doing is maintaining our position. Yet by the time we reach this position of little further advancement we have formed a commitment to the peak - for we have invested our time into climbing to the top and for however little we may receive back at this stage, the peak itself does give us some value for our effort.

It is simple logic to recognise that one's peak is made up of past choices and accordingly there must be many other mountains that we *could* have climbed, each one representing other choices. It is also logical to assume that the current peak we are on is not necessarily the best, the highest, or the one that fulfils our needs in the best possible way. There are many different lives we could have led and there is no reason to assume that we are currently leading the life which would give us the greatest happiness or the greatest fulfilment of our dreams.

Stop now and think about your own peak, your own current position in the plan of your life. What other peaks do you see? There are different types of landscapes and to a large extent your history of how you have in the past engaged with "the edge of chaos" has created the landscape in which you now find yourself.

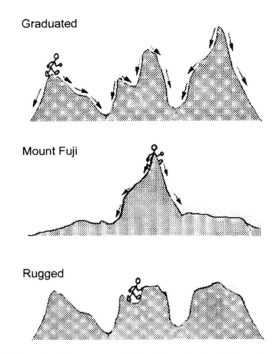

Figure 17 - Three landscapes people build with their lives. A person can live in a graduated landscape with clear pathways to better options. They can live in a Mount Fuji landscape where they think they have no options. They can live in a rugged landscape in which they can see options but have no idea as to which will yield the best results. In these landscapes the valleys represent one way to encounter "the edge of chaos".

If you look out and see peaks which move off into the distance and slowly grow in height, then you live in what is defined as a graduated landscape (*see figure 17*). In a graduated landscape you can see a pathway to better peaks. With appropriate motivation, there is a good chance that you will have the courage to descend from your current position, suffer the confusion, the leanness of resources and/or the difficulties of the valleys in order to begin to climb what appears to you to be a better summit. It is for this reason people willingly go through the upheaval of moving house, changing jobs, ending or starting relationships, and the like, in an effort to move to a distant but better peak. The graduated landscape is the preferred landscape in which to live as it allows you to undertake journeys into the confusion of the valleys with greater confidence. Furthermore, if at a time of transition a supposed pathway does not occur where expected, then because you are moving through a series of graduated peaks, you can quickly recognise a new pathway opening up to higher pinnacles. You are more willing to take risks with what you have *now* because you can see the potential elsewhere which will, in turn, lead to what you consider will be a better life.

People build graduated landscapes by developing the skill to visit "the edge of chaos" frequently and to recognise and harvest the new flickers of emerging order. Some people call this luck but in truth this "luck" is created by people who are willing to take risks and thus find more plentiful opportunities. Such people talk of following their hunches, picking up the "smell" of an option or "keeping their ear to the ground", meaning they seem able to pick up on new incoming order and patterns before the rest of us.

If a person lives in a graduated landscape, what they seek from the astrologer are matters of timing, when to leave one peak and begin the journey of climbing another. They will not generally be concerned with questions of direction or require motivation. Their astrological needs will be different to the person living in other types of landscapes.

Meet "Barbara", a client who lives in a graduated landscape, clearly reflected in her email which I received in January, 2006, along with a request for a consultation[3]:

---

[3] Personal email and quoted with permission.

..I am a physical therapist here in the US, still doing travel assignments which means I work approximately 3-6 months at a time, traveling to different states and working in different facilities. My current assignment (since January) is in Florida, where I am escaping a NY winter.

While I am happy with the travel part - as this is my dream come true - I am always disenchanted with the job itself, because of the paperwork, bureaucracy etc. that always comes first - and the patients wind up being second. This always makes me feel like I can't wait until the job is over and perhaps changing my career path altogether; especially lately.

I have no husband or children - my family is small and spread out with my sister and her kids in Boston and my mother in NY. I am very independent, to a fault sometimes.

My plans for the next 12 months are hopefully to be able to:....

Here Barbara lists five major goals for the year, all of which she is eager to start and which include professional improvement for her career, researching and making some successful investments, buying a small farm so she can start to put down roots, study for personal enjoyment, and winning a forthcoming marathon.

Not surprisingly, her need for a consultation is to gain help with timing and planning. She does not require the astrologer to look for better peaks in her landscape. She wants help with the order in which she should endeavour to scale these new multiple peaks she can already see. Given her natal chart (*figure 18*) are you surprised that she has built herself a graduated landscape?

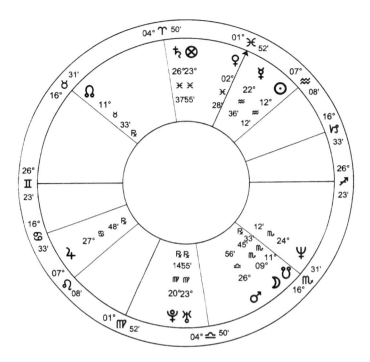

Figure 18 – "Barbara" – birth data not supplied for privacy.

Barbara's mutable angles with Gemini rising and Pisces on the MC suggest a willingness to engage with "the edge of chaos". Added to this, the Uranus, Pluto and Saturn combination squaring the Ascendent shows a major desire to be active and engaged in life, for better or for worse, and with the ruler of the Ascendant (Mercury) forming an air trine to the Gemini rising, Barbara never lacks ideas that feed her powerful pro-active engine room. Barbara is, of course, free to build whatever landscape she desires but her natal chart shows that she can easily generate ideas and act on those new options. Her chart reflects her landscape, so to the chaotic astrologer's eye the consultation can focus on timing and approach, rather than redirection and motivation.

However, sometime a person will find themselves living in what is defined as a Mount Fuji landscape *(see figure 17)*. They discover that they are standing on one lone solitary peak and as they look out from their position, they see no other peaks and thus no other opportunities or options on the horizon. The Mount Fuji individual is the client who may have stayed in their comfort zone for so long that the ripples of new patterns and order have all but disappeared. They see themselves in an unhappy situation but it is a situation they believe they have no chance of changing. When a client lives in a Mount Fuji landscape, they are not seeking a new pathway but rather reassurance that there are actually other options available to them. By focusing on the inherent qualities and potential of their chart and asking the client questions about their routines, habits, patterns and how they may be able to break up some of their habit patterns, the chaotic astrologer can help the client to move closer, in *any way whatsoever*, towards their "edge of chaos", for only then would the client begin to see new peaks emerging.

Look at this email from "John" that I received in January, 2005[4]:

> In 1992 in France (after having obtained my
> "compulsory (parents)" University degree) I started
> a singing-course at the Academy. In June 2001 I
> obtained my diploma and took further private
> lessons with several teachers. To become a profes-
> sional classical singer had been my dream since I was
> sixteen, but I had not enough Mars to fight my
> parents. Now I am too old for conservatory. This has
> made me very depressed and I haven't sung a note
> for over a year now. However, I'd like to start
> practising again. But is there any chance for me to
> get enough "acclaim", so that in the end I might

---

[4] Personal email and quoted with permission.

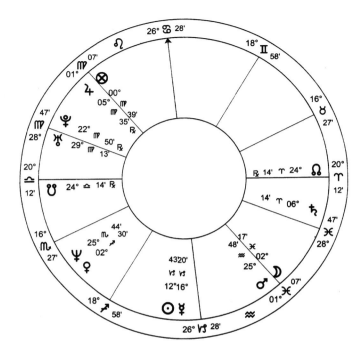

Figure 19 - "John" – birth data not supplied for privacy.

earn my living (or partly) through an artistic career?
It needn't be just classical music.

We can see John's musical artistic nature through the ruler of
the chart (Venus) in a cross sign conjunction to Neptune,
with Neptune forming a trine to his MC (*see figure 19*). There
are many different ways that this combination could have
expressed itself in his life but the dream of a career in singing
is within the nature of this "strange attractor".

Having cardinal angles and a Moon-Jupiter combination
one would not expect John to have avoided the "edge of chaos"
and painted himself into a Mount Fuji landscape. However,
although John is simply asking for a consultation to see when
things will improve for him, within the thinking of chaotic

astrology, and given his potentially active chart, all the chaotic astrologer has to do is motivate him to do *anything*, as any activity whatsoever will start producing new options for him. The timing of predictive events will help him decide the best times to actively engage "the edge of chaos" and a general reading focused on the potentials in his chart can help John to motivate himself to embrace the new emerging order as it bubbles to the surface of his life. In this case the chaotic astrologer really needs to give John the courage to come down off his Mount Fuji peak.

A third category contains those people who have built and live in what is defined as rugged landscapes (*see figure 17*). They stand on one peak and can see many other peaks but all peaks look the same and whilst they can see options, these options seem no better than the peak on which they are currently perched. They are therefore unable to see a pathway forward that promises a better future. Such a client tends to view change with confusion; they do not be seek timing from the astrologer but rather surety about any possible pathway.

"Clare's" rugged landscape is visible from her email which I received in April, 2005[5]:

> I'm not sure that I'm doing what I should be doing
> as far as my job is concerned. I teach disaffected
> young people who have issues such as homelessness,
> drug issues, lack of motivation - many are young
> offenders. Whilst it can be rewarding and I do enjoy
> some aspects of my work, it is also stressful - the
> training company I work for is not supportive; it's all
> about targets as far as they're concerned. Added to
> this is the fact that there have been many redundan-
> cies made recently so I am concerned about my job,
> too. As much as I wonder if I'm in the right job, I
> worry about not having employment. You see, I am

---

[5] Personal email and quoted with permission.

financially better off than I have been for a long
time. I used to work part time at the local college
but left in 2002 because I needed full time work, it's
hard to get full time work there. Now I have been
able to buy my house and am in the process of doing
the whole place up! I don't want my sons to worry
about me also and whilst I'm financially okay and on
my feet so to speak, they are happier, too. So,
getting back to my original topic, I wonder if I
should be doing something else or if I'm doing what
I'm meant to be doing in life?

Clare's difficulty is that she is unhappy with her current peak,
even though she accepts that it gives her value for effort.
However, as she looks out, she is aware that there are other
options, other peaks but cannot judge if they are better than

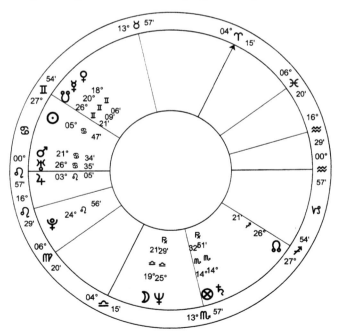

Figure 20 -" Clare" – birth data not supplied for privacy.

her current one, so she is not motivated to encounter the valleys. Such rugged landscapes can actually turn into Mount Fuji landscapes over time, as inaction causes the other peaks in the landscape to dissolve away.

Whilst the Uranus, Mars, Jupiter group around her Ascendant (see figure 20) is an important natal combination which indicates that she is not inclined to slide into the stuck state of a Mount Fuji situation, Clare needs direction. She needs the chaotic astrologer to stand with her on her current peak and point to not one or two but three or more new peaks in the distance. She then needs the astrologer to suggest the best times for her to leave her safe place and encounter "the edge of chaos" in the valleys.

People build landscapes and they live in them but just as they build them, they can also change them. All three clients had reached the top of their current peak. Barbara looks out on a sea of possibilities with clear goals and seeks her next peak to climb, John has found himself on the top of a lone peak that he finds unfulfilling but cannot see any other peaks around him, while Clare accepts the value of her current peak, is aware that there are many other peaks but does not know if another peak would be higher or better than the one on which she stands.

Most clients are at the summit of a peak when they first seek astrological input, as this is the time when they instinctually know they need to make changes. These three examples are simple and whilst there are many other issues in the charts of Barbara, John and Clare, we can see from their emails how willing and open they are to visiting their own personal "edge of chaos". Thus the type of landscape in which they find themselves is an important piece of information as it defines the chaotic astrologer's approach to the whole consultation.

By looking at the client's landscape, one also quickly gains an insight into their history of how they have dealt with visiting "the edge of chaos" in the past. Landscapes can take a long time to build and although the natal chart can help you decide the type of landscape, as in the case of Barbara (*in figure 18*), it is only the client's story which will give you this confirmation. The landscape may match the chart or it may be in tension with the chart, as is the case with John (*figure 19*).

Many astrologers may already carry out this type of assessment of a chart without thinking in terms of landscapes. However, all new solutions to old problems begin with the person's ability to visit their 'edge'. Understanding this and seeing the person's landscape as a map of their past actions gives the chaotic astrologer insights into the best approach to take in terms of forthcoming predictive events. However, whatever the client's situation, the chaotic astrologer also knows that all landscapes can be changed. If you are journeying through a rugged landscape, you may move through a canyon and begin to find yourself in a graduated landscape with clear peaks and pathways. If you have the courage to leave the loneliness of the Mount Fuji peak, you may well find that the clouds lift and reveal other mountains. The aim of life from the chaotic point of view is to frequently visit the valleys of "the edge of chaos" in order to cultivate a graduated landscape. The mountain peaks give us our rewards but we reach them through the valleys of our personal landscapes.

Predictive Work, Saddle Points, Bifurcations and Homeostasis

Bifurcations allow us to change our peaks and chaos theory labels the places where these changes occur as saddle points. When a living system reaches a saddle point, chaoticians indicate that they can predict the nature of the choices being offered but cannot say exactly which pathway will be taken (*see Chapter 4*). This is, of course, the nature of astrological predictive work: a predictive astrologer can indicate the timing of incoming changes as well as the general nature of the changes but most predictive astrologers do not believe that they can predict its exact expression.

Yet, as we have already discussed life is resistance to change, a state called homeostasis. We define homeostasis on a biological level by observing how a species propagates itself: dogs give birth to more dogs, not cats and rabbits. On a psychological level it indicates that a person will inherently seek stability and will resist small change. Many things will happen to you during the course of a day, some planned, some not planned; generally speaking, you will absorb the changes and resist letting them alter your plans. All of us have a strong driving need for homeostasis and it is this drive which can work against us in our need to visit "the edge of chaos". It is also life's love of homeostasis which is the reason that we find making habit changes or changes in life-style so difficult, thus we find the old pattern slipping back into place after a few weeks of effort.

The chaotic astrologer working with predictive techniques is always judging that event's ability to bring notable change into a person's life. This is obvious when we consider the transits of the Moon which sweep through a chart giving all variations to all sensitive saddle points every month. Our need for homeostasis will easily resist such small and frequent events when it comes to protecting our stability. Yet, as we are all too aware, other types of transits or predictive event will indicate that a bifurcation point has been reached and that change will occur.

We met this point when looking at Anne's chart in Chapter Four. Now let us reconsider Barbara's chart (*figure 18*) and the timing of her email.

For Barbara, different saddle points are being activated at this time. Transiting Pluto forms a conjunction to her Descendant (a saddle point) as well as a transiting square to her natal Saturn (another saddle point), while transiting Saturn forms a square to her natal Moon (a third saddle point). There is a lot more to her predictive work than just these transits and a more detailed approach to predictive techniques and delineating predictive work in a client's chart can be found in my earlier work on this subject[6]. However, at this point in time clearly transiting Pluto forming a conjunction to Barbara's angle is going to be the major bifurcation. A person's natal Descendant is a highly sensitive saddle point and the transit of Pluto via this conjunction is a once in a life time event, so we expect this transit to indicate incoming events which will overcome Barbara's natural homeostatic tendencies. Barbara is being presented with the opportunity as well as the pull to "jump" to a new part of her life-fractal. Astrology can clearly define the boundaries of the timing, as well as show the quality of this change. As transiting Pluto tends to indicate irrevocable change to a person's life, we can predict that one of Barbara's five new peaks that she wishes to climb in the coming year will probably take up all her energy and pull her into an unknown place, involving her place of residence (Pluto natally in the 4th house) and her daily work and life pattern (Pluto is the modern ruler of the 6th house); and since transiting Pluto is conjuncting the Descendant, she will probably totally re-arrange her commitments to a group, possibly through her work responsibilities.

Change is coming into Barbara's life and as her astrologer, you would be pleased that she is already contemplating different peaks. Yet apart from the normal

---

[6] Bernadette Brady. (1992). *The Eagle and the Lark – a Textbook of Predictive Astrology*. Maine, USA: Samuel Weiser.

timing and nature of the bifurcation of which astrology is so capable, there is one other thing that the chaotic astrologer can offer Barbara. This additional component comes from blending the findings of chaos and complexity with the practice of astrology and it can be used to show Barbara how to steer a pathway through the turbulence of the bifurcation and even possibly how to help her bias the final results towards her preferred options. To do this we must first look at how a person maintains the order in their life.

Rituals and routines - a way of working with emergent order

One of the challenges of working with the void is the attempt to influence the nature of the new emerging order. We now know that if someone is in a stuck state, a company is in decline or a person's life is grinding to a halt, then new order can be created by increasing the company's relationships between its personnel, or propelling the individual into new social or intellectual situations. Increasing the relationships within a system takes it closer to "the edge of chaos".

This concept in itself is logical but at the same time it is astounding. It leads to innovative companies breaking up their hierarchies by, for example, setting up basketball matches between the staff instead of rigid planning meetings, and then watching for new order to emerge, often appearing as a lucky break or an out of the blue coincidence that "had nothing to do with breaking up the old structure". Nevertheless once the new order emerges, it needs first to be assessed as to its viability and if viable, the company has to be capable of taking a risk to move in the new direction indicated. In business management the fact that complexity has been coined "part physics and part poetry" or "engaging the soul at work" shows the acceptance of this apparent a-causal nature of the applications. But what any company wants is a surer plan, a way of mixing the creative silt of the Nile and obtaining the desired change from the brew in a more structured manner. This is also what we would want for our individual lives: how can we visit our "edge of chaos" and come away with a consciously desired gift? Yet such possibilities seem to be beyond the findings and thinking of complexity and chaos. But are they?

Other cultures in our history have lived and worked with chaos. The ancient Egyptians, like the people of the early Mesopotamian cultures, did not believe that the order they saw in the world could be taken for granted. They did not assume that the sun would rise in the east every morning and the fact that it did from one morning to the next was proof that order, established and formed from the silt of the Nile, was still being maintained. Furthermore, the order that did exist needed to be conserved through the use of ritual. The Egyptians built their temples to house the gods who, for them, were symbols of the world order. In these temples they performed the daily rituals which they believed protected and co-created the precious order of the heavens and thus of the kingdom. Such was the importance of these rituals that the inner walls of the temples or tombs were painted with the acts of these rituals not as decoration but as methods for the perpetuation of the rituals in the absence of a priest[7].

The idea that ritual can co-create and conserve the order of the world is also evident in indigenous myths where story revolves around the relationship between a bird and a tree, or a river and its fish, or a bear and its movement through a forest[8]. Such stories are vital as they ensured the health of the native culture and its environment, both deemed to be one and the same. With their repeating rhythm, day by day, season by

---

[7] see F.Dunand, and C.Zivie-Coche. *Gods and Men in Egypt, 3000 BCE to 395 CE*.
[8] see S.Kane. *Wisdom of the Mythtellers*.

season, year by year, such rituals are a form of self-similarity. Jungian psychologist van Eenwyck actually suggests that the practise of a ritual can be reduced to the simple idea of the iteration of an equation that produces a fractal[9]. He suggests that by considering that time is circular not linear, we can use ritual at seasonal times to remake the world and allow human kind to rejuvenate itself, just as chaos rejuvenates order. This is what lies at the core of pagan seasonal rituals which most of us still perform with the celebration of Christmas and Easter. By collectively performing certain rituals at key times of the seasonal cycle, we are as a culture effectively co-creating the seasonal cycle and helping it move forward in an orderly and predictable manner. We are, in a manner of speaking, helping the Nile stir the silt of the river in the way that we know will produce the desired precipitations of order that underpins our culture and society.

The repeating nature of ritual is an expression of the self-similar nature of life.

Self-similar mornings, self-similar Mondays...

We all use the idea of self-similarity in our daily lives. Think of your morning patterns, your mundane rituals. If you partake of a normal nine to five job, then each weekday morning will involve a pattern. If this pattern is disturbed, you may become agitated, for this is the way that you maintain the order of your day: your morning patterns of ablution, of eating, of greeting others, the transport you take, and so on, are vital. These routines stretch throughout your whole day and involve your travel plans, shopping, food choices and coffee breaks. The list is endless and even encompasses little things like whether you put your left or right shoe on first. Such actions

---

[9] J.van Eenwyck. *Archetypes and Strange Attractors* :113.

are in fact exercises in self-similarity and if they go wrong then we hear comments such as "He got out on the wrong side of the bed" or "I ran out of coffee this morning and since then the rest of my day has gone downhill."

We also know that self-similarity occurs across scale. By maintaining your routines and patterns in the small areas of your life you help to maintain order in larger, more uncontrollable areas of your life. As you maintain the order of your own life you also help to maintain the order of your society's life; wheels within wheels, scale invariance, what happens in one place, small or large, is reproduced at other levels.

You may now want to pause and think for a moment, for what these findings indicate is that the order of your society and the order of your life is directly linked to the order of your personal routine. This is what it means to live inside a fractal-like place. It is for this reason that the Egyptians considered the life of the "silent man" the most divine of all, for this was a man who *always* lived within his personal habit patterns and thus, they believed, helped to maintain the order that was already there.

In the same way today, modern society is maintained by law abiding citizens who work to earn money so they can pay their taxes and be good consumers which in turn co-creates the culture and the society in which they live. Not much has changed in thousands of years; the state still wishes that we live the life of the "silent man" and we still use social rituals to maintain the order of our society.

A creative touch of chaos
So what would happen if you changed something in the order of your day?

We know that any tiny change in a pattern can lead to huge repercussions later in time (the principle of SDIC). We also know that one of the definitions of life is that a living system is resistant to change (the ability to maintain homeostasis). So little changes will not throw you off course; your homeostatic tendencies will endeavour to keep your life running down the same pathway. However, if we make small, repetitive changes in our daily routine at a time when the pattern of a life has reached a bifurcation, then it may be possible to coax a new emergent pattern into life and stimulate it to form a cascading change to the whole pattern.

So just when is your life at a bifurcation point? When it is ripe for change? And if one knows the time when the patterns can potentially change, then what is the right action to be taken at that time to precipitate the desired change?

Barbara's Pluto transit tells us she is approaching a time of change, a time when her natural ability to maintain homeostasis is going to be overcome. She is moving towards or within the influence of a bifurcation, what complexity would call a tipping point in her life. Now since self-similarity in our daily routines and habit patterns helps to maintain the order of our day and the order of our lives and a small change, constantly repeated at one level, will reproduce itself at another level, ask yourself as an astrologer what would happen in this highly charged period of time if Barbara consciously began to change some of her daily routines in a repetitive manner?

If she, say, does her hair differently or stirs her tea in a different direction, she will effectively evoke the principle of SDIC at a key time when new order *wants* to emerge. Furthermore, as she evokes this new order, she can watch for it and then encourage it in her life. In all the chaotic creation myths, the first life that emerges has to help pull the rest of order from the void. Barbara needs to watch for the new ideas or opportunities that she wants and then actively reach down and draw out the tiny first flickers of the pattern as it emerges.

Is this idea of ritual and change of routine a totally alien concept to astrology? No, it is not. Jyotish astrology (Hindu astrology) believes an approaching transit can be directed to a good end by chanting a mantra many thousands of times[10]. Within Jyotish astrology there is a long tradition of recognising the time of a bifurcation and changing one's daily routine in order to help precipitate or cascade a tipping point into a desire outcome. The mantra acts like a drum beat, a regular pulse injected into the person's routine, at a time when they are sensitive to change. Within the logic of chaos theory and complexity, the actual words of the mantra are not important, for the active ingredient is the change of daily habit pattern imposed by the chanting of the mantra. The words of the mantra, however, can become important in that they encourage the necessary mental awareness to look for the right type of changes.

Staying with Jyotish astrology for the moment, let us assume that a person is having a Saturn transit to their midheaven and you, their Jyotish astrologer, have recommended that they chant a Saturn mantra. What you are actually encouraging them to do is to firstly, alter their daily routine in a repetitive manner and secondly, cause them to become selectively perceptive to the smallest flicker of a new Saturnian pattern. You are asking them to do this at a time of an astrological bifurcation when, it is believed, any new patterns will be Saturnian in nature.

This is one of the major concepts of chaotic astrology – the combination of timing, linked to changes to ritual or routine which hopefully stimulate the desired quality of event.

---

[10] James T.Braha,.(1986). *Ancient Hindu Astrology for the Modern Western Astrologer*. Miami, Flordia: Hermetician Press: 72.

For clarity these points are worth summarising as follows:

Find, using predictive astrological techniques, the times of bifurcation or tipping points – this is when change will come into the person's life, the time when they will be visiting "the edge of chaos".

Suggest that the person in this time period change their daily routine in some way in a repetitive manner. This is iteration which helps to produce new order.

Define the quality or the nature of the potential new patterns that want to emerge at this time through the use of normal astrological predictive techniques.

Encourage the person to watch for the first new patterns, via coincidence, serendipity or even synchronicity, of the new opportunities they wish to harvest.

Once the person sees the new patterns, they need to have the courage and the trust to act on the small fragments of opportunities presented to them.

Continuing the example of the Saturn transit, let us assume that the client has a difficult superior at work and they desire a new job with greater responsibility. As astrologers we know that the quality of Saturn transiting the midheaven can indicate either a clash with an authority figure at work or a new job with extra responsibility, or an event of similar nature which falls within the quality of the Saturn transit. What the client seeks of course is the most positive option of the new job opportunity.

This is a possible storyline. As the Saturn transit approaches, the person begins to change their daily routine in a constantly repeating manner (chanting the prescribed mantra or any other activity). Independent of their work issues, the person notes an odd coincidence, for example, a misdirected letter or a wrong phone call, both of which may be for a company to which the person is drawn. Such apparent meaningless coincidences are the flickers of new emergent order drummed up by the beat of the mantra in the person's routine. If this tiny lead is encouraged and acted upon and eventually unfolds into a new job and new career, the person may well shake their head at the awe and mystery of their life, seeing their new life pivoting from the random coincidence of the wrong phone call. What is closer to the truth however is that the person created the opportunities, created the wrong-number which lead to the new job, firstly by their change of habit and then secondly by their mental attitude and alertness in following the lead of the wrong-number to actually seek employment with that new company. The person, with the help of their astrologer, has effectively reached down and scooped the newly forming clump of mud from the silt of the Nile and then, like the Egyptian mythological potter, used it to create their desired object.

So what can Barbara do with transiting Pluto moving over her Descendant?

Firstly, she needs to be clear about what it is she would like to have happen and this desire needs to fall within the boundaries of the nature or quality of transiting Pluto moving over the Descendant. One of Barbara's desires was to buy a small farm so that she could begin to put down roots. With Pluto natally in her fourth house, this desire falls within the transit's nature and if this was to come to pass, it would mean that she would be moving home. So if before the transit started she began to clean out shelves or pack boxes, a little every day, then in a sense she is stirring the silt of the Nile in a particular way. If while doing this if she is also hyper alert to the small flickers of new emerging order – and there will be more than one - so that she can encourage the most appropriate one, then she is engaging fully with the patterns of her life. If she contacted you and said that she was thinking of taking someone to court - also within the nature of Pluto over the Descendant - this would indicate the emergence of the new pattern but a particular expression of the pattern that she may not wish to stimulate and grow, so you may well advise her to not follow through on the court action.

What you put your energy into is what grows in your life. If you are approaching a time of change indicated by your predictive work and you consciously change your routine in some small way which is symbolic of the change that you desire (provided it is within the quality of the predicted change), then you can begin to precipitate the new opportunities that you seek. You then have to watch and seek for the tiny, tiny flickers of the new desired pattern and pour your energy into these small new opportunities.

In the words of the great English novelist Virginia Woolf (1882-1941):

> Let us record the atoms as they fall upon the mind in the order in which they fall, let us trace the pattern, however disconnected and incoherent in appearance, which each sight or incident scores upon the consciousness. Let us not take it for granted that life exists more fully in what is commonly thought big than in what is commonly thought small[11].

---

[11] Virginia Woolf. (1925). The Common Reader 'Modern Fiction'. http://etext.library.adelaide.edu.au/w/woolf/virginia/w91c/ accessed 16 April, 2006

The chaotic astrologer's view of fate

Since life resembles a fractal in its self-similar and scale invariant patterns, the chaotic astrologer is able to view an individual's life like a Persian rug, complex, intricate and beautiful, but also containing predictable elements. The client's homeostatic tendencies will imply that they cling to their own pattern, reproduce the swirls and images of its past. Thus to the chaotic astrologer a client who is resisting change (living within their fractal-like space) will be at a time in their life when events are more clearly defined, more predictable both in the timing and nature of the events, in the same manner as one can look at a Persian rug and predict the timing and shape of the unfolding pattern. Such a client will be following their fated pattern, as discussed in Chapter Five. However, we all reach tipping points (bifurcations in chaos theory) where our life can change in an unpredictable fashion. A tipping point in a client's life is like the Persian rug's mosaic pattern suddenly swirling into new colours with new emphasis.

According to the findings of complexity, the actual nature of the change in the pattern would not be predictable but the chaotic astrologer would not totally agree. To the astrologer the timing of such a tipping point would be flagged by significant predictive events (large transits or progressions or the like). As well, the astrologer would be able to judge the quality or rough nature of the possible new order from the natal chart without seeking total certainty in the predictive work, as the "expected" (the continuation of the pattern) is the very thing that would *not* occur.

This has large implications for the practice of chaotic astrology, for it implies that the client's preferred pathway can be predicted with some measure of accuracy only between tipping points. Consequently the chaotic astrologer could look at the natal chart of an infant and suggest that they will be pulled towards a life of ambition and power. Furthermore, they

could look at the pattern into which the child was born –
family expectations and family resources - and suggest a possible
expression of such an effective or powerful chart, such as a
leader in their circle of society or successfully carrying on the
family business. They could not, however, look at a natal chart
and announce the birth of a "Napoleon". For it is the person's
reaction to these tipping points or bifurcations that would
create the final outcome of their life. One set of choices creates
the life of a "Napoleon" while another by the same chart creates
the story of an ambitious head of a village family.

Therefore, a chaotic astrologer would see a client's life
as containing two types of periods: that of when the person
was living within their comfort zone and that of when they
were moving through a tipping point. It is when the client is
in their comfort zone that predictive work could be done with
greater clarity.

The chaotic astrologer can however use the predictive
tools of astrology to flag the location and nature of future
tipping points and even help the client with actively engaging
with co-creating their future by changing some of their daily
routines at these key times. However, although they could
suggest the quality of the incoming new order the astrologer
would be "blind" to the precise events which unfolded at a
tipping point.

For this is where a person's freewill exists, at the tipping
points of their life. Here they can actively mix their freewill
with the finite choices revealed by the predictive astrology
and create new patterns. Having created these new patterns,
they will once again seek homeostasis and return to a more
consistant and predictable state; the client has to firstly co-
create the new patterns of their future with the void before
the astrologer can begin to read these patterns.

The role of the chaotic astrologer ... a final point

The astrologer will have an inherent understanding of the total unity of all living and non-living systems and will therefore see their client's life as part of that person's unfolding fractal within their family's and their society's history. Within that view the astrologer would also understand both the client's need to maintain the pattern of their life as well as the great sensitivity that pattern has to change at tipping points. Thus the astrologer would know that if they can help the client create a *small* change in their attitude at the right time of their life, then this will lead to *huge* changes, while at the same time they can help the client begin to engage in actively co-creating with the void through repetition and personal daily ritual. However, the astrologer would always be aware of treading lightly, with sensitivity and respect for the client's patterns, as footsteps carelessly placed could precipitate an undesired result from a bifurcation.

In working with chaotic principles the astrologer can also help the client to explore more interesting or fulfilling parts of their own personal patterns and thus consider other landscapes, other peaks, and other options available to them.

As this book draws to a conclusion we can recognise that the domination of logic and order has left us adrift in a reductionist world. In this world we may believe we are in control, but in fact we are reduced to mere spectators wondering at the patterns of our life, with nothing more than a diviner's manual or hope to guide us. However, by adopting chaotic thought into astrology we gain a valuable tool for engaging more fully with these patterns. For chaotic astrology removes us from the role of spectator and places us in the position of the potter at the wheel of our own life. Like the ancient Egyptian creator entity of Khnum we can begin to select the patterns that emerge from the silt of the Nile and shape the clay of our life with our own hand.

Astrologers have been working for a long time to understand how life unfolds. Now according to chaos theory, it would seem that our practice is not so strange anymore.

Astrology can find a home in chaos.

GLOSSARY OF
CHAOTIC TERMS

Attractors - There are three types of attractors:

a) A point attractor - This is a system that moves towards a stable equilibrium, such as a clock pendulum.

b) A periodic attractor – This is a system with a periodic oscillation. The planets orbiting around the sun move around the attractor but do not encounter it.

c) A strange attractor – This is a chaotic system. The behaviour of a particle or object appears to move chaotically. However, when it is analysed, the object is found to be moving around a "moving" foci and the movement or the different positions of the foci create a pattern[1].

See "Phase Portraits" for an overview of the system of attractors, basins, saddle points and SDIC.

Basin – The area of influence of an attractor. With a funnel, this is a point attractor, the basin of the attractor is the funnel's bowl. See "Phase Portraits" for an overview of the system of attractors, basins, saddle points and SDIC.

Bifurcations and Hopf Bifurcations – Points in a non-linear dynamic scheme where changes occur to the behaviour of the scheme[2]. A Hopf bifurcation occurs when a bifurcation fails to stabilise itself, leading to a cascade of bifurcations[3]. Also see *tipping point*, complexity's version of a bifurcation.

Chaos: Deterministic chaos and Entropic chaos - Chaos, as used in chaos theory, refers to deterministic chaos which is used to describe a system that appears random but one in which patterns are rebuilt[4]. In contrast, entropic chaos occurs when all order is lost and none emerges.

---

[1] F. Capra. *The Web of Life: A New Scientific Understanding of Living System*: 132.
[2] R.Abraham. *Chaos, Gaia, Eros*: 66.
[3] J.van Eenwyk. *Archetypes and Strange Attractors*: 61.
[4] ibid:45.

Complexity – A phase membrane which exists between the states of stasis (no change) and chaos (all change). In this phase spontaneous order emerges which increases the complexity in the system[5]. Complexity science works with open systems such as the environment or communities, where the variables cannot be understood or controlled.

Differential Equations - Equations which express certain formulas of constant relationships and in which changes in the value or magnitude assigned to certain variable factors determine the value or magnitude of the other variable factors. These equations are helpful in solving many problems of higher mathematics and the natural sciences because the knowledge of certain known factors permits one to compute the value or magnitude of the unknown variable factors.

Edge of Chaos – This is a place between statis and total change where new order emerges. Despite the name "the edge of chaos", this is not a place where one moves into disorder but rather is a place which can be visited by increasing the relationships or information feeding into a system. Such new input gives rise to a new spontaneous order emerging without an artisan hand. The edge of chaos is the zone where all new order emerges. It is the place of origin.

Entropy – a term introduced by Rudolf Clausius (1822-1888), a German physicist and mathematician, to measure the dissipation of energy into heat and friction[6]. The greater the entropy of a system, the greater the distribution of energy within that system.

Fractals - Fractals are a graph created by plotting the results of equations that are pushed into chaos by what is known as iteration. The result of an equation is fed back into the same equation as the next set of variables. The results of an iterated equation will either move off into infinity or produce order (a closed shape). The results of the order-producing equations are plotted to produce a visual representation which Mandelbrot defined as a fractal. In this way the visually - observed patterns of the fractals are the patterns which are spontaneously formed at "the edge of chaos".

---

[5] see E.Corcoran."The Edge of Chaos"; S.Kauffman. "Antichaos and adaptation" and *At Home in the Universe*; M.Waldrop.*Complexity: The Emerging Science at the Edge of Order and Chaos.*
[6] F. Capra. *The Web of Life: A New Scientific Understanding of Living Systems*:180.

Imaginary numbers - These are numbers which exist outside our philosophy of numbers. For example, the square root 25 is 5 or -5 because in our number philosophy we say that 5x5 = 25 as well as -5x-5 = 25. However, if we seek the square root of a negative number like -25, we cannot answer this question. To resolve this limitation on our number system the idea of an imaginary number was created and the square root of -25 becomes 5i or -5i. Thus imaginary numbers can carry quality as well as quantity as they maintain their positive or negative value. These imaginary numbers play a vital role in physical and engineering calculations, as well as in the generation of Julia and Mandelbrot set fractals.

Imaginary numbers can be combined with real numbers to form what is called complex numbers. The range of complex numbers which do not move into infinity when iterated, can be plotted on a Cartesian plane (graph) to produce a fractal. The complete set of all of these complex numbers that produce a closed pattern is used to create the m-set.

Iteration – From *iter*, Latin for a journey. The process of feeding the results of an equation back into itself and then re-solving the equation. When certain equations are "iterated", they give rise to chaos.

Homeostasis – A unit which is resistant to small perturbations. Attractors provide a homeostatic situation. In a large system the attractor drains a large basin and so changing any one component within this large basin has little impact within the network. However, a unit with a small trajectory and a small basin can be altered permanently by a small change. For example, if you add one white mouse to a population of 10,000 brown mice, the impact on the gene pool is minimum. The mouse population is in homeostasis. However, if you add 2,000 white mice to the same population this will have a large impact on the gene pool and in that situation the population would not be in homeostasis. Any system which does not have homeostasis is considered to be chaotic (moving into unpredictable change).

Lock-in – A term used in complexity to indicate that a particular pattern has a high level of homeostasis by becoming dominant throughout a culture. The QWERTY keyboard is a good example of lock-in. First designed to ensure that letters that were frequently used together in English were not too close on the key board so that their mechanical bars would not jam together, this keyboard, which is considered to be ill designed for human use, is now the universal standard. It has achieved lock-in. We experience lock-in personally when we are dealing with, or trying to change habit patterns. For a habit pattern is a behaviour which has achieved lock-in and when linked with our homeostatic natures it can make a habit pattern most difficult to change.

Phase Portrait – The map which plots or identifies the system's attractors and basins of attraction and classifies them in terms of their topological characteristics. The result is a dynamic picture of the entire system called the "phase portrait"[7] .

A simple example of a phase portrait could be the layout of a golf course with its 18 holes as the attractors to which all the little white balls seem to be drawn. The greens and fairways would be the basins - the area that seems to draw the little white balls towards the attractors. The teeing off area could be considered the saddle points – the place where change will occur. The sand traps and roughs could be the areas of entropic chaos where the little white balls never reappear. The entire golf course plan is the phase portrait of the course. This of course ignores weather conditions and the skill of the golfer, which could be equated to the SDIC factors of the chaotic system.

Saddle Point – The point in the system where a bifurcation can occur. See "Phase Portraits" for an overview of the system of attractors, basins, saddle points and SDIC.

Scale-invariance – The feature of a fractal that produces the same shapes regardless of scale. This is also the feature of nature that produces the same shapes from the micro to the macro. In the human sciences it is the feature of a family's history to be similar to that of a country, the events concerning the family pet reflecting the events happening to the family's finances, and so forth. Self-similarity and scale invariance are, in chaos thinking, the agents which produce the concept of omens, superstition and divination.

Self-similarity - The feature of a fractal that continues to produce the same shapes. In the human sciences it is the feature of a family or a person to experience the re-occurrence of patterns.

Sensitive Dependence on Initial Conditions (SDIC) - Abbreviated to SDIC. A term in chaos theory which states that small changes at the beginning can lead to disproportional results . See *Phase Portraits* for an overview of the system of attractors, basins, saddle points and SDIC. Complexity science does not use the principle of SDIC as complexity

---

[7] ibid:134.

works with open systems where the initial conditions cannot be plotted. However, complexity accepts the impact of a tipping point which is that a tiny local event can potentially have huge global impact.

Structural coupling – The past history of the equation in the way that it has moved through different bifurcations. In human science this can be equated to the history of the subject.

Tipping Point – Named by Malcom Gadwell[8] in 2000, it is the tiny event that occurs locally in a "super-saturated" situation which tips it into a new order for the individual or on a global level. This event could be insignificant and meaningless but it acts as a catalyst that ignites a cascade of change. Complexity science sees tipping points as the time when the whole system changes into a new expression whereas chaos theory which works with closed or semi-closed systems sees these as a hopf bifurcation.

Topology - Topology is the mathematical study of the properties that are preserved through deformations, twisting, and stretching of objects. It studies the "wholeness" properties of an object rather than its parts. One of the central ideas in topology is that spatial objects like circles and spheres can be treated as objects in their own right, and knowledge of objects is independent of how they are "represented" or "embedded" in space. For example, the statement "if you remove a point from a circle, you get a line segment" applies just as well to the circle as to an ellipse and even to tangled or knotted circles, since the statement involves only topological properties.

---

[8] Malcolm Gadwell. (2000). *The Tipping Point: How Little Things Can Make a Big Difference*. Boston, MA: Little-Brown.

BIBLIOGRAPHY

Abraham, F.D., Abraham, R.H., and Shaw, C.D. (1990). *A visual introduction to dynamical systems theory for psychology.* Santa Cruz, CA: Aerial.

Abraham, R.(1994). *Chaos, Gaia, Eros.* New York: HarperSanFrancisco.

Ayala, Francisco (2004) "Teleology and Teleological Explanations" http://plato.stanford.edu/entries/teleology-biology/ Accessed 8 October, 2004.

Bak, Per.(1996). *How Nature Works: The Science of Self-Organized Criticality.* New York: Springer-Verlag New York Inc.

Bateson, Gregory. (1979). *Mind and Nature: A necessary unity.* New York: Dutton.

Bierlein, J.F.(1994). *Parallel Myths.* New York: Ballantine Books.

Blackerby, R. F. (1993). *Applications of chaos theory to psychological models.* Austin, TX: Performance Strategies.

Bonatti, Guido. (1994). *Liber Astronomiae, Part II.* Translator Robert Zoller. Berkeley Springs, USA: Golden Hind Press.

Brady, Bernadette. (1992). *The Eagle and the Lark – a Textbook of Predictive Astrology.* Maine, USA: Samuel Weiser.

——(1998). *Brady's Book of Fixed Stars.* Maine, USA: Samuel Weiser.

——(2001). "2001 Cycles of Growth and Expansion." In *Astrolog,* editor Barbara McGregor. Sydney, Australia: Wellbeing. 5-10.

Braha, James. T.(1986). *Ancient Hindu Astrology for the Modern Western Astrologer.* Miami, Flordia: Hermetician Press.

Briggs, J. and Peat, F. D. (1989). *The turbulent mirror: An illustrated guide to chaos theory and the science of wholeness.* New York: Harper & Row.

Butz, Michael. (1997). *Chaos and Complexity – Implications for Psychological Theory and Practice.* Washington, DC, USA: Taylor and Francis.

Çambel, A. B. (1993). *Applied chaos theory: A paradigm for complexity.* Boston: Academic Press.

Campion, Nicholas. (1982). *An introduction to the history of astrology.* London: ISCWA.

——(1994). *The Great Year. Astrology, Millenarianism and History in the Western Tradition.* London: Arkana.

——(2000). *Astrology, History and Apocalypse.* London: CPA Press.

Capra, Fritjof. (1996). *The Web of Life: A New Scientific Understanding of Living Systems.* New York: Doubleday.

Chamberlin, Roy and Feldman, Herman.(1950).*The Dartmouth Bible*. Boston, USA: Houghton Mifflin.

Copleston S.J., Frederick(1962). *A History of Philosophy* (vol. I, part II): *Greece and Rome*. New York, USA: Image Books.

Corcoran, E. (1992). "The Edge of Chaos". *Scientific American*, 267.A:17-22.

Cornelius, Geoffrey. (2003). *The Moment of Astrology, Origins in Divination*. Bournemouth, UK: The Wessex Astrologer Ltd.

Curry Patrick (1989). *Prophecy and power: astrology in early modern England*. New Jersey, USA: Princeton.

Davies, P. (1989). *The new physics*. New York: Cambridge University Press.

Davies, Paul (2004) "Undermining Free Will" in *Foreign Policy*. Sep/Oct. Issue 144:36.

Dunand, Francoise and Zivie-Coche, Christiane. (2004). *Gods and Men in Egypt, 3000 BCE to 395 CE*. London, UK: Connell University Press.

Ebertin, Reinhold. (1940). *The Combination of Stellar Influences*. Tempe, USA: AFA.

_____(1976). *Directions, Co-Determinants of Fate*. Tempe, USA: AFA.

Frankfort, Henri. (1956). *The Birth of Civilization in the Near East*. New York: Double Day.

Franz, von, Marie Louise. (1980). *On Divination and Synchronicity. The Psychology of Meaningful Chance*. Toronto, Canada: Inner City Books.

_____(1992). *Psyche and Matter*. London: Shambhala.

Friedman.R.E .(1997). *Who Wrote the Bible?* San Francisco: HarperCollins.

Gadwell, Malcolm. (2000). *The Tipping Point: How Little Things Can Make a Big Difference*. Boston, MA: Little-Brown.

Gettings, Fred. (1985). *Dictionary of Astrology*. London, UK: Routledge & Kegan Paul.

Gleick, James. (1987). *Chaos: making a new science*. New York: Viking-Penguin.

Gould, Stephen, Jay (1987). *Time's arrow, time's cycle: Myth and metaphor in the discovery of geological time*. Cambridge, MA: Harvard University Press.

_____(1989). *Wonderful Life: The Burgess Shale and the Nature of History*. New York: Norton.

Greene, Liz. (1984). *The Astrology of Fate*. London: George Allen & Unwin.

_____(1996). *The Art of Stealing Fire*. London, UK: CPA Press.

Gribbins, John. (1984). *In Search of Schrodinger's Cat*. London: Black Swan Books.

Guirand, F. (1965). *Egyptian mythology*. New York: Tudor.

Gunzburg, Darrelyn. (2004). *Life after Grief: An Astrological Guide to Dealing with Loss*. Bournemouth, UK: Wessex Astrologer.

Hahn, Roger (2005) *Pierre Simon Laplace 1749-1827: A Determined Scientist*, Cambridge, MA: Harvard University Press.

Hastings, Nancy Anne.(1984). *Secondary Progressions – Time to Remember*. York Beach, Maine: Samuel Weisers.

Hauskeller, Michael. (2005). "Telos:The Revival of an Aristotelian Concept in Present Day Ethics." In the *Inquiry*, February, 2005; 48(1) 62-75.

Hesiod, the *Theogony* - http://omacl.org/Hesiod/theogony.html Accessed 30 March 2006.

Hillman, James. (1996). *The Soul's Code, In Search of Character and Calling*. Sydney, Australia: Random House.

Holland, John.(1995). *Hidden Order: How Adaptation Builds Complexity*. Reading, Mass: Helix Books.

Holt, Jim. (2006). "Beyond the Standard Model". In the *Scientific American*, April, 2006; 80 – 81.

Hurst, David K. (1995). *Crisis & Renewal: Meeting the Challenge of Organizational Change*. Boston: Harvard Business School Press.

Jervis, Robert.(1997). *System Effects: Complexity in Political and Social Life*. Princeton: Princeton University Press.

Johnson, Robert. A. (1991). *Owning your own shadow: Understanding the dark side of the psyche*. United Kingdom: HarperCollins.

Kane, Sean. A.(1998). *Wisdom of the Mythtellers*. Ontario, Canada: Broadview Press.

Kant, I. (1971). *Kritik der Urteilskraft*. Ed. G Lehmann. Stuttgart: Reclam.

Kauffman, Stuart. (1991). "Antichaos and adaptation". *Scientific American*, 256 (2), 78-84.

_____(1993). *The Origins of Order: Self-Organization and Selection in Evolution*. New York, Oxford University Press.

_____(1995). *At Home in the Universe: The Search for the Laws of Self-Organization and Complexity*. New York: Oxford University Press.

Keepin, William. (1995)."Astrology and the New Physics". *The Mountain Astrologer*. Aug/Sept: 12-21.

Kellert, S. H. (1993). *In the wake of chaos: Unpredictable order in dynamical systems*. Chicago: The University of Chicago Press.

Kepler, J. (1609). *Astronomia Nova*, trans. W.H. Donahue 1992. London:Cambridge University Press.

King, L.W.(1902) 2004. *The Seven Tablets of Creation: The Babylonian and Assyrian Legends Concerning the Creation of the World and of Mankind.* Montana, USA: Kessinger Publishing.

Kirchner, James. W. (1989). "The Gaia Hypothesis: Can It Be Tested?" *Reviews of Geophysics* 27.: 223-235.

Koestler, Arthur. (1959). *The Sleepwalkers. A History of Man's Changing Vision of the Universe.* Harmondsworth, UK: Penguin Books Ltd.

Ladyman, J.(1998). "What is Structural Realism?", in *Studies in History and Philosophy of Science.* 29: 409-424.

Laertius, Diogenes. (2004) *Lives of Eminent Philosophers.* http://www.quotationspage.com/quote/24074.html Accessed 15 September, 2004.

Latour, Bruno.(1991). *We have never been Modern.* Trans. C. Porter. Cambridge, Ma: Harvard University Press.

Leo, Alan. (1923). *The Progressed Horoscope.* New York, USA: Astrologer's Library.

Lewin,Roger. (1992). *Complexity: Life at the Edge of Chaos.* New York: Macmillan.

Lorenz, Edward. (1963)."Deterministic nonperiodic flow", in *Journal of Atmospheric Sciences.* Vol.20 : 130—141.

Lovelock, James. (1979). *Gaia.* London: Oxford University Press.

———(1996). *The Ages of Gaia: A Biography of our Living Earth.* London: Oxford University Press.

Luce, J.V. (1992). *An Introduction to Greek Philosophy.* London: Thames and Hudson Ltd.

Lull, Ramon. (1994). *Treatise on Astronomy.* Translator Shapar, Kris. (editor)Hand, Robert. Berkley Springs, USA. Golden Hind Press.

Mainzer, Klaus. (1994). *Thinking in Complexity: The complex dynamics of matter, mind and mankind.* London: Sringer-Verlag.

Magee, Bryan. (1987). *The Great Philosophers.* London: BBC Books.

Mandelbrot, Benoit. (1977). *Fractals: Form, chance, and dimensions.* San Francisco: W.H. Freeman.

———(2004) "A geometry able to include mountains and clouds" in *The Colours of Infinity.* London, UK: Clear Books: 46-65.

Mansfield, V. (1995). *Synchronicity, science, and soul making: Understanding Jungian synchronicity through physics, Buddhism, and philosophy.* Chicago: Open Court.

Mansueto,Anthony.(1998). "Cosmic Teleology and the Crisis of the Sciences" in *Philosophy of Science.* on-line Journal of papers presented for the Twentieth World Congress of Philosophy, in Boston,

Massachusetts 10 August, 1998. http://www.bu.edu/wcp/Papers/Scie/ ScieMans.htm Accessed 16 October, 2004.

Masha'allah. (1998). *On Reception*. Translator Hand, Robert. USA: Arhat Publications.

Maturana, Humberto. Francisco Varela. (1987). *The Tree of Knowledge*. Boston: Shambhala.

McClure, Mary Ann. (2004). "Chaos and Feminism — A Complex Dynamic: Parallels Between Feminist Philosophy of Science and Chaos Theory". http://www.pamij.com/feminism.html Accessed on 5 October, 2004.

McTaggart, Lynne. (2001). *The Field*. Hammersmith, UK: Element.

Meyer, Michael, R. (1974). *A Handbook for the Humanistic Astrologer*. New York, USA: Anchor Press.

Middleton, C. Fireman, G., Di Bello, R. (1991). "Personality traits as strange attractors". Paper presented at the Inaugural Meeting for the Society for Chaos Theory in Psychology. San Fransicso, CA . pp 19. http://www.societyforchaostheory.org/ Accessed 15 January, 2004.

Morgan, Gareth.(1997). *Images of Organization*. Thousand Oaks, Calif.: Sage Publications.

Morin, Jean-Baptiste. (1994). *Astrologia Gallica Book Twenty-Two Directions*. (Trans) Holden, James. Tempe, USA: AFA.

Neumann, E. (1995). "The origins and history of consciousness". *Bollingen Series XLII*. Princeton, NJ: Princeton University Press.

Olney, James. (1980). *The Rhizome and the Flower, The Perennial Philosophy – Yeats and Jung*. Berkeley, USA: University of California Press.

Parpola, Simo. (1970). *Letters from Assyrian Scholars to the Kings Esarhaddon and Assurbanipal Part 1*. Germany: Butzon and Kevelaer.

Piaget, J.(1950). *The psychology of intelligence*. New York: Harcourt, Brace, Jovanovitch.

———(1952). *The origins of intelligence*. New York: International University Press.

Phillipson,Gary.(2000). *Astrology in the Year Zero*. London: Flare Publications.

Poole, Robert. (1989). "Is It Chaos, or Is It Just Noise?" *Science* 243 (January 6):25-28.

Prigogine, I. (1980). *From being to becoming: Time and complexity in the physical sciences*. San Francisco: W. H. Freeman.

———(1997). *The end of certainty: Time, chaos, and the new laws of physics*. NY: The Free Press.

Prigogine, Ilya, and Isabelle Stengers.(1984). *Order Out of Chaos: Man's New Dialogue with Nature*. New York: Bantam Books.

Ptolemy, Claudius. (1969). *The Tetrabiblos*. (Trans) Ashmand. J. M. Mokelumne Hill, USA: Health Research.

Reiner, Erica. (1999). "Babylonian Celestial Divination", in *Ancient Astronomy and Celestial Divination* (ed) Swerdlow, N.M. London: MIT Press. 21– 37.

Rochberg, Francesca. (1998). *Babylonian Horoscopes*. Philadelphia, USA: American Philosophical Society.

Rudhyar, Dane (1967). *The Lunation Cycle*. Santa Fe, New Mexico: Aurora Press.

Russell, Bertrand. (1961). *History of Western Philosophy*. George Allen and Unwin:UK.

Sasportas, Howard. (1989). *The Gods of Change – Pain, Crisis and the Transits of Uranu , Neptune and Pluto* . London: Arkana.

Segal, Robert. (2004). *Myth, A very Short Introduction*. Oxford, UK: Oxford University Press.

Settegast, Mary. (1990). *Plato Prehistorian, 10,000 to 5,000 B.C. Myth, Religion, Archaeology*. New York: Lindisfarne Press.

Shulman, Helene. (1997). *Living on the Edge of Chaos, Complex Systems in Culture and Psyche*. Zurich: Daimon.

Stillman, Drake. (1996). *Galileo*. Oxford UK: Oxford University Press.

Tarnas, Richard.(1996). *The Passion of the Western Mind: Understanding The Ideas That Have Shaped Our Worldview*. New York : Ballantine Books.

Teller, P. (1998). "Quantum Mechanics and Haecceities", in Castellani, E. (ed.), *Interpreting Bodies: Classical and Quantum Objects in Modern Physics*, Princeton: Princeton University Press.114-141.

Tester, Jim. (1987). *A History of Western Astrology*. Woodbridge, UK:The Boydell Press.

Trungpa, C. (1991). *Orderly Chaos: The Mandala Principle*. Boston, USA: Shambhala.

van Eenwyk, John. (1997). *Archetypes and Strange Attractors*. Toronto, Canada: Inner City Books.

Varela, Francisco. and Maturana, Humberto. (1980). *Autopoiesis and Cognition*. Dordrecht, Holland: D.Reidel.

Walker, C.B.F. (1989). "A sketch of the development of Mesopotamian astrology and horoscopes." in *History and Astrology*. (ed) Kitson, Annabella. London: Uwin Paperbacks. 7-14.

Walker, E. H. (2000). *The physics of consciousness: Quantum minds and the meaning of life*. Cambridge, MA: Perseus.

Waldrop, Mitchell.(1992). *Complexity: The Emerging Science at the Edge of Order and Chaos.* New York: Touchstone.

Weaver, Warren.(1963). *Lady Luck, the Theory of Probability.* Harmondsworth, UK: Pelican Books.

Wheatley, Margaret J.(1994). *Leadership and the New Science: Learning About Organization from an Orderly Universe.* San Francisco: Berrett-Koehler.

White, Andrew D. (1897). *A History of the Warfare of Science with Theology in Christendom.* London, UK:D. Appleton and Co.

Wieland-Burstanm J. (1992). *Chaos and order in the world of the psyche.* England: Routledge.

Williams, Bernard. (2001). "Plato – The invention of philosophy". in Monk, Ray., Raphael, Frederic (eds). *The Great Philosophers.* London: Phoenix.

Willis, Roy., Curry, Patrick. (2004). *Astrology Science and Culture, Pulling down the moon.* New York: Berg.

Wing. R.L. (1979). *The I-Ching Workbook.* New York: Doubleday.

Woolf, Virginia (1925).The Common Reader 'Modern Fiction'. http://etext.library.adelaide.edu.au/w/woolf/virginia/w91c/   accessed 16 April, 2006.

Young, Arthur. (1976). *The Reflexive Universe: Evolution of Consciousness.* New York: Delacorte Press.

Further References

Anon 2004:1 - Australian Aborigine myths
http://www.dreamscape.com/morgana/miranda.htm#AUS
Accessed 30 September, 2004.

Anon 2004:2 - Chinese myths
http://www.dreamscape.com/morgana/ariel.htm#HAW
Accessed 30 September, 2004.

Anon 2006:3 - Fractal landscapes
http://ata-tenui.ifrance.com
Accessed 26 March, 2006.

INDEX